Leadership
and the Force of Love

Leadership
and the Force of Love

Six Keys to Motivating With Love

JOHN R. HOYLE

CORWIN PRESS, INC.
A Sage Publications Company
Thousand Oaks, California

For information:

Corwin Press, Inc.
A Sage Publications Company
2455 Teller Road
Thousand Oaks, California 91320
E-mail: order@corwinpress.com

Sage Publications Ltd.
6 Bonhill Street
London EC2A 4PU
United Kingdom

Sage Publications India Pvt. Ltd.
M-32 Market
Greater Kailash I
New Delhi 110 048 India

Printed in the United States of America

Library of Congress Cataloging-in-Publication Data

Hoyle, John R.
  Leadership and the force of love: Six keys to motivating with love /
  by John R. Hoyle.
     p. cm.
  ISBN 978-0-7619-7870-1 (c.) — ISBN 978-0-7619-7871-8 (pbk.)
  1. Success. 2. Leadership. 3. Love.   I. Title.
  BJ1611 .H712 2002
  158'.4—dc21   2001003982

This book is printed on acid-free paper.

10   11   12   13   14   7   6   5   4

Acquiring Editor:	Robb Clouse
Associate Editor:	Kylee Liegl
Corwin Editorial Assistant:	Erin Buchanan
Production Editor:	Olivia Weber
Editorial Assistant:	Ester Marcelino
Typesetter:	Marion Warren
Cover Designer:	Michael Dubowe
Indexer:	Teri Greenberg

Words of praise for
Leadership and the Force of Love

In most of today's organizations, the fusion of love and work is an oxymoron. But top-performing teams and businesses such as Motorola and Southwest Airlines credit love as a crucial ingredient in their success. Love is caring and compassion, something today's schools need more than standards and high-stakes tests. Hoyle's book provides both a wake-up call and a roadmap for leaders to follow in bringing love and work together.

—TERRENCE E. DEAL
Irving R. Melbo Professor of Education
Rossier School of Education
University of Southern California

In this wonderful new book, John Hoyle writes about the one four-letter word that leaders most avoid but should not—love. Hoyle shares his understanding that the quickest way to the head is through the heart and that leaders who can't love, can't lead. This is a book that anyone who thinks of themselves as school leaders should read and by doing so, believe.

—PAUL HOUSTON
Executive Director
American Association of School Administrators

This powerful message comes at just the right time. We are indebted to John Hoyle for sharing his refreshing perspective on educational leadership and school reform that focuses on the worth and dignity of everyone involved.

—MARTHA MCCARTHY
Chancellor's Professor
School of Education
Indiana University

This heartwarming book is vintage Hoyle—filled with insight and joy, the message is clear—love, you can't lead without it! A must-read for every member of your administrative team.

—THOMAS J. SERGIOVANNI
Lillian Radford Professor of Education and Administration
Trinity University (TX)

John Hoyle has written a powerful and very readable book about the force of love in producing champions in sports, business, education, and government. His real life stories and examples are filled with advice, humor, and inspiration to jump-start your leadership efforts. A must-read for your management team and friends.

—GENE STALLINGS
Head Coach, 1992 NCAA Football National Champions
University of Alabama

The book Leadership and the Force of Love portrays a powerful message. Dr. Hoyle delivers a unique and proven approach to leadership. By de-emphasizing the theories of leadership and focusing on the actual behaviors of successful leaders, this book will help all audiences gain an understanding of why effective leaders that incorporate these concepts are known by what they do—not by what they say.

—BEN D. WELCH
Director, Center for Executive Development
Mays College & Graduate School of Business
Texas A&M University

Contents

Preface

During my many years of conducting seminars for leaders in education, business, agriculture, and government, I discovered a strong undercurrent of King Kong mentality. Reactions by managers to my presentations and team-building activities are riddled with comments about ways to control employees by rewarding the best and shooting the rest.

Among those comments are the following:

- "My employees are so dumb it takes them two hours to watch *60 Minutes.* Watch them every minute."
- "You can't win the Kentucky Derby with a mule. I have to threaten to fire them every day to make them work."
- "I tried to be a team builder for a few years until I realized that loyalty to my organization is only a seven-letter word. I now employ search-out-and-destroy methods."
- "Doc, you just don't understand today's workers. You can't show kindness because they [the workers] will take advantage of you."
- "You are preaching to the choir, professor; our bosses in Washington or Dallas are the ones who need to hear about team building and love."
- "My people are cynical about another management fad coming from on high. I have quit talking about continuous improvement, 'principle-centered' leadership, vision, and empowerment, and I never talk about love."

How do you react when hearing a presenter talk about trusting employees, empowering workers, site-based decision making, and unconditional love for others in the workplace? Have you ever said, "You can't count on anyone today. You have to watch out for old number one"? Why have we become so cynical in our organizational lives? Our parents, teachers, and religious figures told us to share, trust, and love others.

Since the turn of the 20th century, authorities in management and leadership have attempted to lead us away from the boss-led side of scientific management espoused by Frederick Taylor to the human side of the enterprise led by Mary Parker Follett, Chester Barnard, Douglas McGregor, Rosabeth Kanter, Stephen Covey, Tom Sergiovanni, Terry Deal, and many others. Although these writers have influenced many organizational leaders to transform their leadership and management styles, much remains to be done. Distrust, fear, dishonesty, and abuses of power in organizational life are realities in schools, businesses, government, law enforcement, and universities.

I have taken the leap to "go there" to address these maladies that continue in organizations. I have attempted to go beyond the concepts of leading with heart, soul, and morals and have moved on to the concept of love in an attempt to reteach the lessons of history's great leaders that can renew organizations. As you read this book, you will revisit ideas that guide human kindness, social justice, and servant leadership and discover ways to replace anger, mistrust, and hatred with love. By using the force of love to guide your daily interactions with others, you can transform the way you do business and gain a self-respect that may have been lost in your journey to success.

I cut to the chase in Chapter 1 with "If you can't love, you can't lead." This is not some statement of a hopeless romantic. There is nothing romantic about my argument claiming that without love in organizations, violence, intolerable stress, and poor quality will continue. Increased competition as a survival mode in business, high-stakes testing in schools, and greater demands for accountability in medicine, food processing, and universities will continue to breed isolation and discontent unless love guides ways of organizing. The type of love I espouse for this book is unselfish, loyal, and benevolent concern for the good of another. The Greeks used the word *agape* as the highest form of love. Agape is unselfish love. It is self-giving, not self-seeking. This chapter explores liability in love, how to love unlovable people, parental love and teenagers, and how love overwhelms hate in the workplace.

Chapter 2 introduces the first key to motivating with love—vision. You will learn more about the power of vision in your own life and in successful organizations, how vision led Jack Welch and others to greatness in leadership, and the connection between service and vision. Chapter 3 explores ways to communicate with love and move others to high performance and the keys to becoming a persuasive speaker. "Teamworking With Love" (Chapter 4) includes a self-report to check your teamwork skills, the art of praise over blame, and the case of the Barbie Doll Drill Team. Chapter 5 walks you through ways to empower others with love and provides examples of how abusive power destroys, how empowerment builds, and how kids in Eatonton, Georgia, were empowered by wildlife biologist Liz Caldwell.

The discussion on mentoring with love in Chapter 6 presents steps to mentoring; research about mentoring men, women, and minorities; and the story of how a football coach mentored a quarterback to lead his team to the first conference championship in more than 50 years. The final chapter offers advice and steps to evaluate others with love. You will read about assessment centers, continuous improvement, and the good and bad aspects of high-stakes testing in education at all levels. The chapter also introduces models for evaluating organizations and people in them and ends with an inspiring message by Mother Teresa.

As you begin this book, my hope is that the words will call you to be more caring and to let love rule your comments and the tough decisions you make in your daily work and personal life. The words of the Wizard of Oz to the Tin Man who needed a heart sum up the heart of this book.

"And remember, my sentimental friend, that a heart is not judged by how much you love, but by how much you are loved by others."

Acknowledgments

I wish to thank my spouse, Carolyn, for her editing and patience with me during the long hours of cloistering in my workroom to complete this book. In addition, my coworker Bill Ashworth has performed his magic once more in making the manuscript presentable to Robb Clouse of Corwin Press. I thank Robb for his faith in my ability to write about love for an audience much broader than education and for his efforts in giving wide exposure to the book. I am grateful to Joe Schneider and Paul Houston at the American Association of School Administrators for inviting me to deliver a featured address about this book at the 2001 National Conference on Education in Orlando, Florida. And finally, to all my students who have loved me when I didn't earn it—I thank you.

About the Author

John R. Hoyle specializes in leadership development, team building, and future studies. He has written or edited several books and has produced more than 100 articles and book chapters on organizational and leadership issues. One of his books (coauthored with Fenwick English and Betty Steffy), titled *Skills for Successful 21st Century School Leaders* (1998), is in its third edition and is one of the most widely used textbooks in the field of educational administration. Hoyle's Corwin Press book, *Leadership and Futuring: Making Visions Happen* (1995), remained on the World Future Society's best-seller list for five years. He has served as President of the National Council of Professors of Educational Administration, was chosen as the American Association of School Administrators Professor of the Year, and chaired the AASA National Commission on Standards for the Superintendency in 1993. He has been labeled an educational futurist in interviews by *U.S. News & World Report, Omni Magazine,* and *USA Today.* He is Professor of Educational Administration at Texas A&M University, where he teaches classes in future studies, critical thinking, organizational theory, and program evaluation and holds two university awards for teaching. A popular keynote speaker and workshop consultant, he works with schools, universities, agricultural agencies, the Department of Defense, law enforcement, and businesses in the United States and abroad. A student athlete at Texas A&M University, he spent several years as a teacher, coach, and administrator in the public schools and has taught in five universities and in Europe. He holds a Ph.D. in education and social science from Texas A&M University. In 1999, Hoyle received the first Living Legend Award at the National Conference of Professors of Educational Administration at Jackson Hole, Wyoming.

1

If You Can't Love, You Can't Lead

Let no one who loves be called altogether unhappy. Even love unreturned has its rainbow.

—James Barrie, quoted in *Roget's International Thesaurus*, 1961, p. 614

"What is this love stuff? People need to be told what to do, and if they don't do the job—fire them!" This statement by a CEO in the communications business unfortunately represents the sentiments of many bosses in business, higher education, public and private schools, medicine, agriculture, government, and law enforcement who are concerned only about the bottom line. Today's society has reached such a state—sociologists are calling us the "cynical society" (Goldfarb, 1991)—that it is increasingly difficult for us to talk about love and the essential role that it must play in a democratic society. But my colleague Robert Slater believes that talk about it we must, because it is the nature of modern capitalistic democracies that they increasingly breed isolation, anomie, and discontent. Slater states,

> Love is the most powerful force we have to correct these self-destructive tendencies. So let me be clear at the outset. I do not want to turn attention to the problem of love in human organizations because I am a hopeless romantic. On the contrary, there is nothing at all romantic about my argument. It is based on the hard realities of modern society. (Hoyle & Slater, 2001, pp. 790-791)

Mathematician Bertrand Russell sensed that the *love* word was usually avoided in human discourse when he wrote,

The root of the matter, if we want a stable world, is a very simple and old-fashioned thing, a thing so simple that I am almost ashamed to mention it for fear of the derisive smile and wise cynics will greet my words. The thing I mean is love. (Seymour, 1979, p. 70)

The *love* word is tossed about rather liberally in our daily conversations. We love ice cream, skiing, sports, music, and doing nothing. We love the Rocky Mountains, clear streams, golden eagles, and fishing. Next, we love our friends, teammates, church family, hometown, and school. Most of all, we love our spouses, our children, our parents, our grandparents, and other family members. And for the young at heart, "Love Is a Many Splendored Thing."

Defining Love

For the intent of this book, the best definition of *love* is found in *Merriam-Webster's Collegiate Dictionary* (1993). Love is

(1) strong affection for another arising out of kinship or personal ties; . . . (2) attraction based on sexual desire: affection and tenderness felt by lovers; . . . (3) affection based on admiration, benevolence, or common interests; . . . (4) unselfish loyal and benevolent concern for the good of another. (p. 690)

The fourth definition is the focus of this book. The Greeks used the word *agape* as the highest form of love. Agape is unselfish love. It is self-giving, not self-seeking. Agape love means loving people who are unlovable and who do not give love in return.

Liability in Love

Perhaps Robert Greenleaf (1991) is on target by writing,

Love is an undefinable term and its manifestations are both subtle and infinite. But it begins, I believe with one absolute condition: unlimited liability! As soon as one's liability for another is qualified to any degree, love is diminished by that much. (p. 38)

Most organizations, however, according to Greenleaf, are designed to limit liability for employees. "Keep your distance and never get to know persons well" is all too often the unwritten law of organizations. These "boss codes" of behavior make it easier to reprimand, control, or lay off employees.

Love, then, is a deep caring for others. The people and things we love make life worth living. Love is a mother's heart being melted by the hug of a child and a handmade Valentine card with the words "I Love You Mom." Love is a university student affairs administrator relentlessly pushing her staff to organize and execute freshman orientation week and telling them, "Thanks, I love each one of you for who you are." Love is what we feel for fine music, art, food, and stimulating conversation. We love what we do in business, law, law enforcement, medicine, education, plumbing, nursing home care, food processing, politics, and government.

Poet Elizabeth Barrett Browning wrote, "How do I love thee, let me count the ways," whereas Paul the Apostle told us that "love suffers long and is kind; love does not envy; love bears all things, believes all things, and endures all things." Roman poet Virgil sums it up by writing, "Love conquers all things." Stephen Covey (1990) ranks love as the first of five dimensions to quality of life. He writes, "People need to have a sense of belonging and to be accepted, to join with others in common enterprises, to engage in win-win relationships, and to give and return love" (p. 297). Love is expressed in various ways and with differing levels of meaning.

When a beautiful granddaughter whispers to her grandfather, "I love you, Paw Paw," when a coach says that he or she "loves those kids," or when a couple renew their marriage vows after 50 years with a kiss and an "I love you," love takes on different meanings. Love has been expressed as compassion, fondness, desire, and attraction and is grounded in a person's character, morals, values, and heart. If love is the answer, what is it? What are the links between self-respect, love, and love for others? What are the relationships between love, character, morals, and ethics? How do we lead with the heart before the head? How can we love our way to high standards? Why are we often reluctant to develop a covenant of trust and love with others in our community, to commit to their well-being and support them as much as possible?

Kade and Brady Lane were lucky to have a dad, Dennis Lane, who loved them and held them accountable for their actions. The late Dennis Lane lived through his boys by involving them in Little League, soccer, football, and track. If the boys were around a ball, Dennis was nearby. He was a model dad who lived the right way and touched the lives of his boys and hundreds of young people during his years in teaching and coaching. One of Lane's coaching friends, James Giese, said this about him: "Love stuck out all over Dennis. He loved the world, he loved kids, he loved life, he loved the game. I don't think there was a kid who wouldn't run through a wall for him in the shot, in discus, or on the football field" (Cessna, 2000, p. I5).

In the *Dialogues of Plato*, Diotima said,

> For wisdom is a most beautiful thing, and Love is of the beautiful; and therefore Love is also a philosopher or lover of wisdom, and being a lover of wisdom is in a mean between the wise and the ignorant. . . . For you may say generally that all desire of good and happiness is only the great and subtle power of love. (Jowett, 1871, pp. 224-225)

Love is also caring. Catherine Marshall, Jean Patterson, Dwight Rogers, and Jeanne Steele (1996) write about the difficulty of school administrators demonstrating care in a system that is based on organizational structure, rules, policy, and socialization theory. Schools are organized around strategic plans, goals, objectives, and specific outcomes.

People have defined roles to play in ensuring that policies are carried out in ways to produce systemic change for the better. This concept of *tight coupling* often becomes alien to cooperative planning, decision making, and family building. Tight alignment of the system or school curriculum with the vision or mission of the school system and school is a key factor in improving test scores, but with regimentation and extreme pressure to produce higher test scores, love and caring can disappear from the schools.

According to Marshall et al. (1996), caring

> emphasizes connection through responsibility to others rather than to rights and rules. It involves fidelity to relationships with others that is based on more than just personal liking or regard. An ethic of caring does not establish a list of guiding principles to blindly follow, but rather a moral touchstone for decision making. (p. 278)

Love and the ethics of caring are not merely the words of a dreamer longing for a Camelot workplace. To the contrary, love and acts of caring are the power behind every successful person or organization. Philosopher and theologian Pierre Teilhard de Chardin views "love and energy as being interconnected, suggesting that love contains within it an energy that can unite human beings because it alone joins all of us by what is deepest within ourselves" (Dyer, 1998, p. 227).

Viktor Frankl (1984), survivor of the Auschwitz death camp, agrees with Teilhard de Chardin that love connects human beings like no other force. Frankl reflects on the horror of his three years of starvation and brutal treatment and how he used the power of love to help him forgive and survive. He writes, "Love is the only way to grasp another human being in the innermost core of his personality. No one can become fully aware of the very essence of another human being unless he loves him" (p. 116).

Love is not easy to describe, but we understand it when we see a supervisor using kind and supportive words to an employee who has made a mistake, an eighth-grade teacher staying after school to help a student learn the mysteries of geometry, a truck driver stopping to help a stranded motorist, a doctor calling patients' homes to check on their progress, a police officer serving as big brother or sister for a troubled youth, or a child helping another child who is different—that's love.

Love Ignored

Lee Bolman and Terry Deal (1993) extol the virtues of ethical decision making by managers and the importance of caring for the corporate family with more soul, compassion, and understanding. Tom Sergiovanni (1992) stresses both professionalism and virtue in building school communities through moral leadership, which emphasizes service to others and making schools places of respect and devotion to doing the right things the right way. Stephen Covey (1990) reminds us of the "inviolate principles." He believes, "To the degree people recognize and live in harmony with such principles as fairness, equity, justice, integrity, honesty, and trust, they move toward either survival and stability on the one hand or disintegration and destruction on the other" (p. 18). In *Leadership and Futuring: Making Visions Happen* (1995), I emphasize that a vision for the future must be grounded in selflessness and a personal covenant to helping others succeed.

Caring for others is paramount for organizations to reach their potential. Each of these writers provides valuable insights into examining the hearts and character of leaders. Writers for centuries have inspired us to lead with heart, soul, integrity, kindness, vision, and equity, but only a few have focused on love as a leadership force and the implications for love in the act of leadership (Autry, 1992; Malone, 1986; Marcic, 1997; Sanford, 1998).

Some People Are Difficult to Love

How do we as leaders in organizations express love for others yet maintain professional relationships? Some people are difficult to love, and others fail to respond to love because they have never really experi-

enced it. Managers who experience the ugly side of people and the quix-
otic behavior of others can become cynical and give up any thought about
leading with love. To fight the daily battles of the bottom line, politics,
bigotry, selfishness, greed, hostility, violence, red tape, and loneliness,
administrators need self-love and unconditional love for their adversar-
ies and advocates. When we allow seething anger to control our emotions
and verbally attack unlovable people, we lose.

The old saying holds true: "When you throw dirt, you lose ground."
Corporate executives, small-business owners, and university presidents
can strive to create compelling visions, flawless strategic plans, continuous improvement strategies, and world-class technology, but if "they
have not love," for all customers or clients, their leadership will never be
realized. According to Brownlow (1972), love is "an art more dependent
on heart feeling than eyesight and ear hearing. We cannot fathom people
unless we have the love that feels for them and with them" (p. 72). Love
means forgiveness for people who make mistakes—sometimes serious
ones.

My late father, Jess Hoyle, was an insurance salesman for more than
30 years with Home State Insurance, an Oklahoma company that merged
with American General in the 1960s. He was a leader in sales year after
year and served several years as a staff manager responsible for eight or
nine other agents.

Dad was well-known as a dedicated, honest, fun-loving, competitive
person who did not suffer fools gladly. One of his agents working in the
Claremore, Oklahoma, area was a natural-born salesman who liked the
nightlife and living beyond his means. When Dad did his frequent staff
audits to determine the number of lapsed policies and the amount of
money collected from policyholders, he noticed several hundred dollars
missing from his "party man" from Claremore. Dad's first thought was to
call Home State headquarters and the local sheriff to report the deficit
and to protect his own reputation. Tough love led Dad to his delinquent
agent, however, who told the truth when confronted. After throwing a
barrage of heated words at the agent, Dad then listened carefully to his
explanation. He told my father that he lost money gambling and, when
threatened by collectors, took company money to protect himself and his
family from harm. He explained that he was going to pay it back so that
no one would know.

With tears steaming down his face, the repentant salesman said, "I am
sorry that I let you down and did such a dishonest thing; will you ever be
able to forgive me?" Dad forgave him and gave him a personal loan to
help pay back the money. The next day, the agent got a second job and
paid back the loan in eight months with interest. Within two years, this

troubled salesman led the entire company in policy sales and had the fewest policy lapses by customers. For the next decade, he remained the leading salesperson and made a comfortable living the right way.

The last time that Dad visited him, the agent was in the hospital. In his final moments, the agent told Dad that he was his hero. In this case, love was the answer that saved the career and self-esteem of a champion salesperson for Home State Insurance. Leaders who know the force of love go the extra mile to help individuals who have stumbled. They live the words of Max DePree (1989): "Leaders don't inflict pain, they bear pain" (p. 11).

Great Leaders Who Loved

Love has been the greatest force in human history. Since ancient people formed families and communal groups, love has provided the strength to survive and prosper through tumultuous times of war, famine, disease, prejudice, and ignorance. Psychologist Eric Fromm wrote, "Love is an active power which breaks through the walls which separate people. Love overcomes the sense of isolation and separateness, yet it permits you to be yourself" (Nichols, 1962, p. 65). Poets, theologians, and social scientists ponder the force of love and its mysterious hold on the mind and behaviors of individuals.

The Dalai Lama, Tibetan high priest, believes that love brings tranquility and hope to humanity. He says it this way:

> If there is love, there is hope to have real families, real brotherhood, real equanimity, real peace. If the love within your mind is lost, if you continue to see other beings as enemies, then no matter how much knowledge or education you have, no matter how much material progress is made, only suffering and confusion will ensue. (Singh, 1998, p. 329)

The most powerful leaders of world history are remembered not for their wealth or position but for their unconditional love for others. Jesus of Nazareth, St. Francis of Assisi, Clara Barton, Albert Schweitzer, Frederick Douglass, Mahatma Gandhi, César Chávez, Martin Luther King Jr., Mother Teresa, Billy Graham, and Nelson Mandela stand out among world leaders who stressed love and nonviolence to bring justice and hope to marginalized people. Constantine, Joan of Arc, Winston Churchill, Franklin D. Roosevelt, and George Patton used military force to allow love to rule over hatred, genocide, and totalitarianism.

Dave Moore, a high school teacher and coach in Lenoir City, Tennessee, let love rule after the Columbine and other school shootings by creating the Care Club. The club helps spread love and a deep sense of caring for all students in the school. Before the Care Club, the typical cliques of jocks, freaks, preps, rednecks, and freshmen sat in the cafeteria in their own little groups. Now, with the leadership of Coach Moore, the students intermingle, respect each other, and overlook the differences. Associated Press writer Martha Aldrich (2000) quoted a star athlete whose attitudes were changed because of the Care Club. He said, "Last year, nobody would leave their little circle. This year, people learned to move from group to group. It's like, if you dress different, who cares? If you listen to different music, who cares?" (p. D2).

Tough Love for Success

Managers and administrators are often viewed as inflexible rule enforcers who rarely empower employees to help make decisions that affect them. To avoid conflict with these bosses, employees will usually seek the status quo and continue to do the same old things in the same old ways, finding little joy in the process. Effective managers express love by really caring about their employees through helping them succeed both as persons and as productive workers who reach their goals. In addition, love can mean firing a person who is not successful in a job role.

According to Buckingham and Coffman (1999),

> If the person is struggling, it is actively uncaring to allow him/her to keep playing a part that doesn't fit. . . . Firing a person is a caring act. . . . Great managers move fast to confront poor performance, but also they are adept at keeping the relationship intact while doing so. (p. 210)

Love must be tough when employees, military personnel, students, athletes, and musicians either are incapable of higher performance or must learn the skills through rigorous teaching and, when necessary, stern mentoring. The love that Marine drill instructors express for their trainees is far different from that of kindergarten teachers for their students.

A sales manager facing quotas from the district manager will express love for his or her salespersons with a sense of urgency, whereas a research scientist will express love for lab assistants by pushing them to complete experiments in time to provide funding agencies information that may extend the research grant for another year. Hospital administrators have a difficult time expressing love when caught between the pressure to turn a profit through shorter hospital stays of patients, the demands by insurance companies, and doctors who frequently disagree with the administrative policies.

Parental Love and Teenagers

Parental love usually goes unrecognized by children, especially when they reach the teenage years. Rebellion and newfound answers to everything leave loving parents wondering what happened to their sweet, obedient children. Several years may pass before the offspring will acknowledge the love and sacrifices made by the parents. Most of us are remorseful for the missed opportunities to tell our parents how much we love them. Why is that?

During my senior year in high school in Tulsa, Oklahoma, my father was in the hospital with an extended illness, my brother and I both were wearing casts from football injuries, and my sister was expecting a child and living with us while her husband was in the military. The family income was barely adequate to pay the rent, feed the four of us, and keep our older model Chevrolet running. I remember my brother and I being unkind with our remarks about not having new clothes, a new car, and money for dates. Of course, rather than find a job, I continued playing sports and contributed nothing to the family income. Through the years, I have regretted that decision and my selfish attitude. In my last talk with mother as she lay in the hospital, I told her what a remarkable mother she was and how much I loved her for holding our family together during those difficult years. Such love is what parents give, and we can return it only to our children.

Love Overcomes Evil

Love for others has cost some leaders their lives. Dietrich Bonhoeffer, a German theologian during the rise of Nazi Germany, paid the ultimate price by speaking out against Adolf Hitler and his regime. Hitler's "final solution" was mass extermination, and the final solution of Dietrich Bonhoeffer was love. Bonhoeffer was imprisoned and executed by the Nazi machine for speaking out against the atrocities of the Third Reich. His stand for his religious beliefs and for love instead of the murder of innocent people, expressed in his letters from a concentration camp, left a lasting legacy for the power of love over evil and hate.

Nobel laureate Elie Wiesel was only 15 years old when he, his family, and other Jews were arrested and transported in cattle cars to Auschwitz while most of the civilized world stood by. He asserts that the "opposite of love is not hate—but rather, indifference" (Schleier, 2000, pp. 17-18). Jan Karski, who survived capture and brutal beatings by the gestapo, let love guide him to alert the West about the Holocaust. Wearing disguises and using fake documents, he entered the Izbica and Treblinka death camps to record the horrors of the Nazi war machine. After several close calls with the Nazis, he reached the free world to tell President Roosevelt and others his story. Karski's devotion to others in need drove him to risk his life for strangers because it was the decent thing to do.

Rosa Parks sought love over evil by refusing to take a seat in the rear of the bus. Her act of defiance over an evil law struck a blow for her people, for civil rights, and for the United States. Evil can take its toll in organizational life as being dishonest, hiding information, ignoring the efforts of others, demeaning or diminishing the contributions of others, and sabotaging the leadership and goals of the organization.

Daisy Bates chose the force of love to defeat bigotry by leading nine black students to integrate Little Rock (Arkansas) Central High School in 1957. This bold act opened the door of opportunity for nine students and began changing the minds of school and political officials about equal opportunity for all the children and youth of Arkansas and throughout the United States.

The Loveless Workplace

Lack of love in the workplace is the reason that the comic strip "Dilbert" is so popular. Love in offices, assembly lines, cubicles, classrooms, and chat rooms is a rare commodity in times of pressure by stakeholders for more production, quality assurance, higher test scores, increased accountability, and higher profits. Lack of love at home, school, and work is the reason behind broken homes, violence, shoddy products, high stress, and staff turnover. Love cannot overcome all human frailties and irrational acts. When disturbed individuals take weapons to the schoolhouse or workplace for planned or random attacks on others, love is helpless. In work sites where love and respect are the culture and the way of treating others, however, violent acts are much less likely to happen.

No organization, regardless of its supportive culture and love, is immune to conflict among individuals. Max DePree (1989), quoted earlier, is one of America's leading corporate executives who built Herman Miller,

Inc., into one of the top 25 firms on the *Fortune* 500 list. He believes that love and the "awareness of the human spirit" are more important than structure or policy. He has been successful because he knows that "without understanding the cares, yearnings, and struggles of the human spirit, how could anyone presume to lead a group of people across the street? In modern organizational jargon, person skills always precede professional skills" (p. 221). Organizations that place production over people may have their "day in the sun," win the coveted Baldrige Award, and make the *Fortune* 500 or some other prestigious list, but when profits come hard and performance wanes, management should not cast the first stone at the employees. Managers should get in touch with their own human spirit to reach the heart and soul of their employees.

Self-Respect and Love

"I don't care if they love me or not, but I want their respect" is heard around the workplace by managers and administrators afraid of losing control of their employees. Leaders use technical, interpersonal, and organizational skills to lead others to be dedicated employees and good performers. Is it love or respect that causes a secretary to stay after hours to help the boss meet a deadline? When CEOs of corporations make tough decisions that require downsizing the workforce, do they worry about losing respect and love from those employees given pink slips? When high school or college coaches cut the squad, do they lose respect and love from those young people who had dreams of playing on the team? Some coaches use unloving tactics to cut their squads.

Ten Days of Hell at Junction

In 1954, Paul "Bear" Bryant became the head football coach at Texas A&M College. He brought with him a winning reputation and a legacy of a survival-of-the-fittest training regimen for his players. That first August, Coach Bryant loaded 100 players on two buses bound for Junction, Texas, the site of a barren rock and grass, burr-covered practice field.

It was here that Bryant would separate the men from the boys. The stories of the 10 days of hell at Junction are legendary. The two- and sometimes three-a-day practice sessions conducted in brutal heat with no drinking water during practice caused dehydrated players to collapse or crawl to the sideline. The blocking and tackling drills bordered on brutality, and those unwilling to continue the punishment soon began leaving for home in the middle of the night, some without telling Coach Bryant. Several of the best athletes left because of injury or personal problems with coaches and players.

When the long 10 days ended, 29 players survived, including Gene Stallings, Jack Pardee, and Dennis Goehring. Stallings recalls the survival:

> Those of us who stuck it out ended up staying in Junction for 10 days, 10 of the longest days in my life. I wished a thousand times we would leave the place, but quitting football simply was not an option. It is now history that we went to Junction in two buses and returned to campus in one, and that bus was about half full. (Stallings & Cook, 1997, p. 49)

These three and the others experienced nine losses and one win that fall season. Ten of the Junction survivors, however, became the nucleus of the 1956 team that won the Southwest Conference title. With few exceptions, those who survived have great respect for Coach Bryant. Others cut from the squad during the 10 days of hell in Junction have other opinions about "the Bear."

When decisions are made that affect the future of others, few coaches and managers are immune to pressures related to "playing with the lives of others." Despite flat and more decentralized organizations in which decisions are made closer to the action, administrators make the final decisions to hire, remove, or transfer personnel. Personnel decisions make or break managers of all sizes of organizations. If managers center their personnel decisions on being loved by all concerned, they are in the wrong position. The focus should be on ways to maintain self-respect as a leader while building respect for each member of the organization.

Creating Heroes in Every Role

Creating an environment in the workplace that matches the person with the job and challenges each employee to excel is the shortest route to building self-respect in the corporate, agency, or educational world. This act of leading others to self-respect is grounded in love for them, their families, and the organization.

According to Buckingham and Coffman (1999), top managers must "create heroes in every role. Make every role, performed at excellence, a respected profession. . . . Great managers envision a company where there are multiple routes toward respect and prestige" (p. 184).

Schools are the best example of limited opportunity for advancement of personnel. Strapped with a single salary scale and little hope of promotion to administration, teachers can feel frozen in place for an entire career. Leading school principals and superintendents are aware of this condition and attempt to build in cash incentives for professional development, creating specialized master teachers, department chairs, head teachers, and members of the school and district site-based, decision-making committees. Every effort by the manager to "create heroes in every role" is an expression of love and self-respect.

Respect and love made a difference in the job efficiency and attitude of a person in a low-prestige, minimum-wage job in Pryor, Oklahoma. Elma is a quiet high school dropout, a single parent working long hours in an assisted living center. Her job is to clean floors and remove soiled bedding and diapers of older, frail adults. Each day, Elma reported to work and did what was required to keep her job until the manager gave her the title of "caregiver" to the residents in the assisted living facility. Elma was presented an attractive engraved name tag with her name and new title. The manager told her that the role she played was vital in improving the quality of life for the residents because her warm smile along with the clean linens and clothing she provided made them feel better about themselves as human beings in a sometimes dismal environment.

In a few days, visitors and residents saw a change in Elma's work habits. They noticed Elma's quiet love being expressed for these elderly residents and the pride she took in making each resident feel loved and respected through her kind and friendly attitude toward each person—even the difficult ones. Elma's self-respect and professional pride lifted the spirits and work performance of others in the center as they daily observed her selfless efforts to make life better for those who had lost self-respect and hope.

Leading With the Heart First

Legendary basketball coach John Wooden led with his heart to win—NCAA titles. He constantly told his players, "Every day, try to help someone who can't reciprocate your kindness" (Brown & Spizman, 1996, p. 147). Drs. William Schwartz, Elliot Shubin, Subha Ashlad, Denise Gonzales, Walter Gaines, and John Sarconi, along with nurses, social workers, and others, volunteer to serve less fortunate patients at the Samaritan House Medical Clinic in San Mateo, California. They are sharing their busy lives to keep the clinic open to provide medical and dental services for laborers and families with no health insurance. In an age of managed care and expensive health care, it is a labor of love for these good Samaritans. These angels of mercy are recruiting other retired medical professionals to staff the clinic for no salary or fringe benefits. At the Samaritan House Medical Clinic, Dr. Elliot Shubin, 58, explains, "We come here to practice our profession and to practice our love" (Ryan, 2000, p. 18).

Leading with the heart revealed the wonder of love for Mitch Albom (1997), author of *Tuesdays With Morrie*. Many years after college graduation, Albom rediscovered his favorite professor, Morrie Schwartz, and found that he was dying with amyotrophic lateral sclerosis (ALS). Morrie faced his demise with a dignity that changed the heart of Mitch Albom. Albom began visiting his beloved, dying professor every Tuesday to learn the true meaning of life. On the first Tuesday, Morrie said, "Mitch, you asked about caring for people I don't even know. But can I tell you one thing I'm learning most with this disease?" "What's that?" replied Mitch. "The most important thing in life is to learn how to give out love, and to let it come in" (p. 52).

Giving out love means leading with the heart over the head. Managers with heart manage to outproduce managers who lead with their heads. Fifty years of research and best practice concludes that through the fat and the lean years, managers who place the welfare of employees over the bottom line not only will survive but will lead the industry. Love is more than a word in high-performing schools, corporations, and other organizations.

> *Try to bring a rainbow to someone's life every day. What sort of legacy will we leave? What will they put on our tombstone? I want mine to read that I made a difference in somebody's life.*
>
> —Grace Kremer, quoted in
> Brown and Spizman, 1996, p. 21

2

Visioning With Love

Service providers need a vision of work that is worth believing in, a vision that challenges them, provides emotional energy, and generates commitment.

—Leonard L. Berry, 1995, p. 21

The Power of Vision

Inspirational visions have driven humankind to create magnificent cities, monuments, and art: Rome, Constantinople, the Parthenon, the Pantheon, St. Peter's Cathedral, Michelangelo's *David*, and Maya Angelou's novels. Visions are created by inspired individuals who lead others to share the vision. Visions that lift the spirits and hopes of others must be deeply felt and easy to recall.

James Kouzes and Barry Posner (1996) tell us that visions can be like jigsaw puzzles—when the pieces do not fit, show your people the picture on top of the box. For a vision to stick, a leader must continue telling and showing others how the vision will drive individual and organizational success. According to futurist Joel Barker (1992), "Most leaders are not visionaries. But all leaders know who the visionaries are and select from them, the great ideas that they want to lead to" (p. 169). Benjamin Franklin, Thomas Edison, Mary Parker Follett, and Buckminster Fuller stand out as visionaries who changed the future. Mary Parker Follett's (1930) vision guided her to challenge the grip of scientific management on early 20th-century industry. She believed managers should treat workers with more dignity and change the workplace from strict authoritarian control over workers to a more collegial team concept. Her vision was guided by love for workers who were being used as chattel by corporate managers.

Follett's vision can be seen and felt today when an organization initiates transformational or principle-centered leadership. Years later, Tom

15

Sergiovanni (1992) added to Follett's beliefs by writing, "The management values now considered legitimate are biased towards rationality, logic, objectivity, the importance of self-interest, explicitness, individuality, and detachment" (p. 27). Sergiovanni argues, "These values cause us to neglect emotions, the importance of group membership, sense and meaning, morality, self-sacrifice, duty, and obligations as additional values" (p. xiii). Both Follett and Sergiovanni remind us that love guides successful organizations. A vision without love can lead to disaster. Remember Adolf Hitler's vision for a "thousand-year reign"?

Service Vision and Fred Brown's Success

Fred Brown's import automobile dealership in Bryan, Texas, is highly successful because love for people supports its vision of service. When customers walk into the showroom or the service department, they are treated like royalty. Fred Brown and his employees dress for success and greet every customer with a smile.

Ron Elms, a sales leader for Fred Brown, says, "The three keys to our success are very clear. One, when a customer walks into the showroom, we focus on what they want, not what we want to sell them. Two, when the customer makes a selection, we give them a fair price up front. Three, our service department lives its name." Fred Brown's service manager, Ron Miller, has what Leonard Berry (1995) calls a service vision. Ron Miller strives to satisfy each customer with his winning way. This service vision is pervasive from the service desk to the mechanics, which explains the high percentage of return customers. Elms continues, "These three keys separate us from other dealerships." Fred Brown's staff "talks the talk and walks the walk," which accounts for numerous national awards for quality customer service. Vision and love for others make miracles happen.

Vision and Motivation

Abraham Lincoln had a vision driven by love when he issued the Emancipation Proclamation, freeing four million slaves; Anne Sullivan used her love-driven vision to teach Helen Keller to talk and live a rich life; in 1851, Sojourner Truth, an uneducated former slave, took the podium at a national convention on women's rights and delivered her famous "Ain't I a Woman" speech. Sojourner Truth's powerful speech detailed her vision for equal rights for black women and helped open more doors for her race and for all women.

Mrs. Shunantona, my seventh-grade math teacher in Wewoka, Oklahoma, had a love-driven vision for me that changed my life. Mrs. Shunantona was short and round and always wore bright clothes to enhance her Native American complexion. She was a no-nonsense teacher who literally pushed me and other students to excel in mathematics. I was not her prize pupil—far from it! I hated math and practically everything that had to do with school. My world as a skinny seventh grader was centered on surviving football practice. After moving to Wewoka, I decided to go out for the ninth-grade football team. I was a sight to behold in a football uniform.

During that summer in 1947, I grew from an attractive, normal-sized, coordinated teacher's pet in the sixth grade in Pryor, Oklahoma (I was so smart in math that I got to dust erasers on the sidewalk once a week!), to a gangly, pimple-faced, awkward six-footer weighing only 106 pounds. My feet grew to size 11, and when I turn turned sideways, I looked like a double *L* walking around. Changing from the best athlete to the worst in three months was a bitter pill to swallow for a kid driven by peer approval.

I was competing with the eighth and ninth graders to make the ninth-grade football team as an end. Coach Miller issued me the last uniform available. Although others had close-fitting white practice pants, a red jersey, well-fitting cleats, and a snug-fitting helmet, I got baggy khaki pants with sewed-in pads, a ragged white jersey with holes in the front that read "Property of Wewoka Junior High," shoes that were two sizes too big with loose cleats that hurt with every step, and socks that slipped to my heel. The greatest insult was the old leather helmet so big that every time I got hit, I was looking through the ear hole!

My role as a football player was blocking dummy. The first team ran a single-wing offense that required four blockers to clear the way. I was placed in their way—all 6 feet 2 inches, 106 pounds of me. Each time I stood in harm's way, the shoes went one way, the helmet the other. After each beating, I would drag my frame home and slip in without my mother seeing the scrapes and bruises. Her response was always the same—"Well, when are you going to quit taking that abuse?" I was not about to quit and risk ridicule of my new friends. Besides, it was all I had going for me in my life during that fall so long ago. Mrs. Shunantona was on my case for not doing my math homework and for my frequent, disruptive comments to a kid named Tommy "Lame Brain" Leamy on the next row. I was a kid who needed attention and was going about getting it my way. Mrs. Shunantona tried to reach me and appeal to my serious side, but I couldn't and wouldn't hear her. Football was on my mind.

The first game of the season was with Holdenville, and I got to suit up. My uniform was unchanged, but I was proud to be on the bench for all to see. During the first quarter, we were driving for a touchdown when Coach Miller called my name! I ran up to this god in my life and said, "Yes, coach?" He said, "Hoyle, give your shoulder pads to Billy; his just broke." I did as ordered, but my night of pride quickly faded as I sat on the end of the bench like a plucked chicken with no future. The team continued to defeat and shut out all opponents. The day before the final game with the Shawnee Wolverines (the high school team was the Wolves), I got a red jersey with the number 9 in white on the front and back. My picture in that jersey was in a prominent place in my parents' house for the remainder of their lives. I looked like a tall waterbird in a football uniform. Anyway, we were clobbering Shawnee, and everyone had played but me.

With 20 seconds to go in the game, Coach Miller yelled, "Hoyle, get in at left end." I grabbed my big helmet and must have been singing "One Moment in Time" as I raced toward the huddle. As I neared the huddle, my left toe caught my right heel, and the rest is a blur. My helmet went spinning across the field, and I crawled to recapture it. Just as I stood up with the helmet in place, I heard a gun fire. "Game's over," screamed the referee.

I looked around toward the stands, which must have held 50,000 fans—well, at least 250. I saw Grandmother, Mother, Dad, snotty-nosed classmates who would give me grief, and my girlfriend, Jean—although she didn't know she was my girlfriend. (The next Valentine's Day, I bought her some candy, but I was too bashful to give it to her and ran around the corner of the building and ate it!) Every person who counted in my seventh-grade life saw my defining moment on that football field that night. I was destroyed with no hope of repair. Should I run away or merely disappear into thin air?

The next morning, Mother woke me and told me to get ready for school. After I told her that I was not going and that I was sick, she urged me, "Get up, and I will iron your jeans the way you like them, and your favorite shirt is clean." I remained under the covers in my cocoon, refusing to reenter the world. After two more calls and no response, Mother brought the switch, and I got up and went to school and to Mrs. Shunantona's math class. I recall entering her classroom just as if it were yesterday. As I walked in head down, Mrs. Shunantona reached up and placed her arm around my skinny neck and said, "John, you had a hard time in that football game last night, didn't you?" "Yes, ma'am," I replied. I said to myself, "Go ahead and kill me by telling the class what a failure I am."

In a loud voice that still rings in my ears, she said, "Boys and girls, before we start the math lesson, listen up; I saw John Hoyle play first base on the junior police team last summer, and I believe he is the best first baseman I ever saw. Please be seated, John." This leader who chose love over ridicule saved my life. I was so lifted that I would have tackled calculus and trigonometry that day if Mrs. Shunantona asked me to. I became her best math student by year's end and had a new handle on my self-esteem.

In two years, I made first team in football and made my grades. Three years later, I received a full baseball scholarship to attend Texas A&M University, passed freshman algebra, and became the first in my family to earn a college degree. A great teacher, Mrs. Shunantona had the vision with the love to do the right thing at the right time to inspire me in that classroom in 1947. Mrs. Shunantona lived the words of Kahlil Gibran (1964): "The teacher who walks in the shadow of the temple, among his followers, gives not of his wisdom but rather of his faith and his lovingness" (p. 56).

Passion and Vision

Jack Welch, former CEO of General Electric (GE), had the passion, wisdom, faith, and love for others to create a vision that went far beyond a strategic plan. His love of life and pioneering spirit attracted other pathfinders to join him in the quest for unexplored territory in technology. He created a vision that gambled with the future of GE by becoming a player in the world market of technology. Welch became known worldwide as a winner and competitor by assuming the mantle of *transcompetition*. Robbins and Finley (1998) write,

> Transcompetitive behaviors are not an abandonment of the competitive ethic but a refining of them, a peeling away of the cultural layer of untrue truisims competition comes wrapped in, that we cheerfully accept, such as, competitiveness is the same as competence—it isn't by a long shot. (p. xi)

Welch worked to make the vision clear about GE's purpose, and his strategy was to drive the vision by hiring competent people to produce quality and outcreate competitors around the world. His vision gained momentum when he purchased RCA, the first of a long line of acquisitions that inspired competitiveness (Tichy & Devanna, 1990).

Miami Heat Coach Pat Riley knows a lot about risk taking to succeed. Succeed he has, by coaching four teams to NBA titles in his 18 seasons. Riley sees no safe path to victory. He says, "I like playing on the edge, and when you reach that proverbial fork in the road, you have to make your move decisively" (Collie, 2000, p. 110).

There is never any doubt about Riley's passion to win, and he drives his players to the brink of exhaustion to hone their skills and beliefs to make them champions. Riley wins the devotion of his players by exuding a tough but loving demeanor in the demanding world of professional basketball. Within each player is the heart of a champion who has caught the Riley vision.

Four-time Olympic gold medalist swimmer John Naber tells about the vision and passion he needed to be a champion.

> One of my favorite sayings I got off a soda bottle: NO DEPOSIT NO RETURN. To me that means you'll get out of life about what you are willing to put in. All champions have made some great sacrifices to win their victories. So when someone talks to me about their goals and dreams, I ask them one question: "What are you willing to do about it?" (Brown & Spizman, 1996, p. 4)

Willie Davis, former Green Bay Packer All-Pro, used visualization before each game to drive his performance. Davis's personal vision and performance led him not only to membership in the NFL Hall of Fame but also to become owner of several companies and radio stations and a member of several distinguished boards.

Attracting Others to Your Vision

Doesn't everyone like to be around people who are enthusiastic about an idea, program, product, or just life itself? Such persons exude confidence, competence, and, above all, hope in an often hopeless world. When these lovers of life share their vision, others listen even if they believe the vision is a pipe dream. Visioning is an exciting process to move people to imagine new and challenging opportunities. The past no longer predicts the future, nor will the future be any more predictable in 10 years. The past will never catch the future and become the "good old days." The good old days exist only in our minds, and few of us would re-turn to them if we had the opportunity.

You cannot drive safely by looking in the rear view mirror, nor can you lead an organization by emphasizing past successes. A cartoon by Gary Larson shows the biblical figure Noah standing on his ark talking to the animals about loading procedures. Noah says, "All right, let's do this alphabetically." The zebra looks up at Noah and says, "Damn." We obvi-ously must learn from the past, but no one will follow a leader who lives there. Leaders with vision lift our hopes for a better tomorrow and hold our hands to venture into the unknown. The known is not exciting, only a memory of what could have been. Vision offers hope. It keeps the human spirit alive and inspires us to climb another mountain, to seek another challenge, and to sign a mortgage on a house.

The key to visioning is the enthusiasm and optimism by you, the leader of the organization. If you are excited about opening new markets, expanding your products, winning the national title, and keeping a com-petitive edge, then others may also catch the enthusiasm and get on board. No organization has ever succeeded without a visionary, nor has any sculpture been completed without the sculptor. When the sublime genius Michelangelo accepted the commission from the Medici family to carve *David* from a marble block, he is reputed to have said, "I accept this honor only because I see David trapped in the stone, and I will free him."

It starts with you and your intellectual and emotional strengths, gaz-ing into the blocks of the future and chipping away everything that doesn't fit your vision. Your role is to take others to places that they have never been and would not go without your vision. The strategic vision is the dynamic to inspire others to take a look and to lead them to uncharted territory. Because there is no road to the future, pathfinders must be in-spired with the mysteries of opportunity that lie ahead.

On D-Day, June 6, 1944, 120 U.S. paratroopers under the command of General "Jumpin'" Jim Gavin were the first to land at Normandy. General Gavin and his pathfinders were inspired by a vision for victory and a love for their buddies and country to risk their lives to place markers around drop zones at Utah Beach for the full-sail American paratrooper and glider assault that would begin one hour later. Although only 38 of these 120 pathfinders landed on target, they carried out their mission to help launch the greatest seaborne invasion force in the history of the world (Davis, 1978).

Gavin and his men made that historic jump because of a man who also had a vision—Adolf Hitler. This strange-looking man discovered that by loud and fanatical speeches, he could make people hate the things he hated. While in prison in 1923, Hitler wrote about his vision to restore Germany to power and his methods for the annihilation of Jews and other non-Aryans in his book *Mein Kampf.*

The world paid little attention to this poorly written recipe for violence and destruction until Hitler's perverted vision led to the death of more than six million innocent persons and destroyed the economy of Europe. His evil vision died on April 30, 1945, in a Berlin bunker when he shot his wife and himself to death.

The Vision Within

The vision within individuals stimulates the intellectual and creative corners of the mind. Architect I. M. Pei's mental model of a pyramid structure to cover the entrance of the Louvre in Paris brought wrath from Parisians who heard about the modernistic monstrosity planned for their most treasured art gallery. Although some remain troubled, most have realized that the pyramid cover makes it possible to enlarge the gallery and increase the efficiency in admissions. Bill Gates chased his vision from his garage to the megastructure called Microsoft. His vision enticed other entrepreneurs to cast their futures with Gates, many of whom became multimillionaires.

The world's greatest male ballet dancer, Rudolf Nureyev, choreographed each graceful movement in his mind before every performance. Ludwig van Beethoven wrote beautiful music although he was deaf. His genius and mental imagery enabled him to create original music that still stirs the heart. Margaret Fuller, a transcendentalist writer in the 1840s, wrote about equal rights for women in American life. Her works challenged the male domination over women in higher education and society. Fuller died before her vision could be realized, but her works led the way toward greater opportunities for women.

Ernest Hemingway's classic novel *The Old Man and the Sea* is rich with imagery inspired by biblical symbols and sports heroes. The imagery is strengthened by the strong tie of love between the old man and the boy he taught to fish. President John F. Kennedy had a vision that changed our world forever in 1960 by declaring that the United States would have a man on the moon by the end of the decade. His vision inspired the nation to raise funds, select and train astronauts, and lift our pride. Unfortunately, President Kennedy did not live to see his vision happen in 1969. A crazed assassin in Dallas had his own vision on November 22, 1963.

At age 16, Winston Churchill had a personal vision of someday speaking eloquently to members of Parliament. He wanted desperately to be like his statesman father and to win his love. Young Churchill's vision led him to visit his family doctor about his speech impediment—a slight lisp. The doctor told him to forget about the lisp because as a soldier, he would be not a speaker but a fighter. Winston kept his vision, overcame the lisp, and is remembered for his powerful, persuasive speeches.

After Churchill's appointment as prime minister, his words before the House of Commons became his best known: "I have nothing to offer but blood, toil, tears, and sweat: you ask what is our aim? I can answer in one word: Victory—victory in spite of all Terror" (Rogers, 1986, p. 75). Churchill's inspiring speeches strengthened the resolve of the British to fight on during those dark times. The people were inspired by his vision for a brighter day and his love for England.

My brother, Jay Hoyle, had a vision that was a source of concern for our parents. During his boyhood, Jay had suffered a serious knee injury playing football and was recruited by the choir director at Will Rogers High School in Tulsa, Oklahoma. The director discovered Jay's powerful singing voice, and the entertainment world gained a star. Our parents wanted Jay to be a gospel singer, but he had another vision to sing and entertain on the stages in Las Vegas, New York, and London. Today, Jay is living his dream as a leading entertainer on the world's finest cruise ships. Our parents finally understood why Jay ran around all night and slept all day—he was merely following his dream to entertain at night and sleep all day.

When Gerald Anderson became superintendent of the Brazosport (Texas) Independent School District, most Hispanic, African American, and white students from lower-income homes were not succeeding academically. During Anderson's first week, he asked his administrators and teachers why these students were unsuccessful. The common response was, "Well, we do the best we can; these kids come from poor homes with parents who place little emphasis on school performance. It has always been this way here." Anderson refused to accept the status quo because his personal vision for students in the Brazosport schools was that "all children can learn."

He began visiting the classrooms, talking to teachers, students, parents, and community leaders about the achievement problems. Armed with a strong understanding of mastery teaching strategies and aligning the curriculum with the test, Anderson incorporated strategies from the Baldrige criteria for continuous system improvement and clearly stated his vision that "all Brazosport students can learn." His belief that children from poor homes could succeed at the highest levels transformed the district to become "exemplary" in only three years. In Texas, to reach the exemplary level, students in the entire school district must master 90% of all academic material as measured by the Texas Assessment of Academic Skills (TAAS).

Anderson used his experience and grit gained as a Marine pilot to institute a "no excuse" policy for all administrators and teachers in his district. His determination to overcome years of bias about the intellectual abilities of minority and poor children was driven by love for his kids. He proved that it could be done, and in 1999, the Brazosport district was selected as one of the two school districts for the national Baldrige Award. Numerous other school districts in Texas and around the world are using the Brazosport model that Gerald Anderson inspired and helped create. One person's vision driven by love can move mountains and help poor kids learn at the highest levels.

Improving Our Serve

Charles Swindoll (1991) writes, "How desperately we need to improve our serve" (p. 11). No, Swindoll is not trying to help our tennis game; he is talking about how to become a better servant leader. Some look at servitude as slavery or being of low stature in society, whereas others believe that having a servant's heart is the greatest talent of all. Swindoll warns us about charismatic, winsome charlatans who are self-centered and claim to be servants to others. The images of Wall Street, the ministry, corporations, education, politics, and other organizations have scars inflicted by wolves in servants' clothing. These corrupt insider traders, self-centered TV evangelists, unethical CEOs in business and education, and bought politicians who fake their service vision to take advantage make it more difficult for true servants.

True servant leadership is guided by a delicate balance between love for oneself and for others. Peter Block (1993) believes that authentic service leadership is experienced when the following occurs:

- There is a balance of power. People need to act on their own choices. Acts of compliance do not serve those around us or the larger organization.
- The primary commitment is to the larger community. Focusing constant attention on the individual or a small team breeds self-centeredness and entitlement.

- Each person joins in defining purpose and deciding what kind of culture this organization will become. We diminish others when we define purpose and meaning for them, even if they ask us to do so.
- There is a balanced and equitable distribution of rewards. Every level of the organization shares in creating its wealth and expanding its resources. When an organization succeeds in its marketplace, money and privilege need to be more evenly distributed among levels if our commitment to service is to have any integrity. (p. xxi)

Many *Fortune* 500 companies follow Block's description of authentic service. Hewlett-Packard's service vision is to hire service-driven employees who have the heart and ability to act on their own in behalf of the company. Management works with all employees to establish state-of-the-art professional training to keep their transcompetitive edge, and employees help build a corporate culture that brings meaning to them and a service-beyond-self work ethic. Hewlett-Packard employees also benefit from corporate profits by opportunities in stock options and other benefits.

Servant leadership must be embedded in love for others. A servant's vision and love are not something shared with a select few. My wife, Carolyn, and I enjoy feeding the birds from our backyard feeder. Each spring, we watch for the beautiful cardinals, finches, and other feathered marvels. Our bird-watching is frequently interrupted by invasions of big aggressive blackbirds that run off our invited guests. One Saturday morning, after repeated assaults by the aggressors, Carolyn placed a dish towel over the feeder. Soon, one of our pretty little guests circled the feeder with a puzzled look and flew away. At that moment, Carolyn came to the realization that offering service to only a select few is not being a true servant leader. The dish towel was removed from the feeder for all birds. Next time, we will buy a larger sack of bird feed.

Improving our serve depends on follow-through. A vision driven by love for every employee is the first step in setting the stage for self-motivation. The follow-through, however, makes the vision happen. Frederick Herzberg (1968) and his predecessors in motivational research found that we really cannot motivate anyone but ourselves.

Motivation is a complex mix of internal drives, needs, urges, and dreams that moves individuals to behave in different ways. No coach, manager, teacher, writer, or psychiatrist ever motivated anyone to do anything! They merely help create the conditions that enable others to find purpose in the goals they seek. Assisting others in creating a mental picture of success is basic to self-motivation. Research conducted with students of all ages reveals that those who have a healthy focus on future success not only make better grades but also finish higher education and move into better jobs than do students with little or no focus on their future.

The importance of visioning in shaping lives is apparent in successful people and those who struggle in school and in the world of work. Because 80% of prisoners are high school dropouts who never created a mental image of a successful life, the power of a personal vision is obvious. Greater emphasis on the visioning process in schools, homes, and other social institutions is necessary to help individuals develop hope for their futures.

When capable individuals fail to live up to their own or others' expectations, a cloudy or missing personal vision is a key reason. Positive role models in the lives of children, youth, and adults remain significant in their building dreams of the future. The first responsibility of management is to inspire employees with a shared vision that motivates them to contribute to its fulfillment in both corporate and personal success. All winning organizations have senior leadership that sets high standards, coaches others to succeed, and never tires of sharing the vision and telling others how important they are in making the vision happen.

Summary

How do love and vision create servant leadership exemplified by Fred Brown, Ron Elms, Ron Miller, Mary Parker Follett, Mrs. Shunantona, Jim Gavin, Gerald Anderson, and others? Vision guided by love is centered first on the welfare of individuals and second on the organization and its strategic plan. Strategic plans are not worth the binders that hold them if they are not inspired by a vision that guides individuals to strive for quality products and pride in accomplishments.

As administrator or manager, how do you transform your organization from the traditional line and staff model that dates from Moses to one that shares power and exudes love and respect for diversity and collaboration? The shift from boss managing to team managing is not easy to make without rethinking the purpose of your organization. In both profit and nonprofit organizations, victory comes only when teams believe in their core values and work together with a passion for excellence. The following suggestions have proved to build success in all types of organizations worldwide:

1. *Rely on a power greater than yourself to guide your vision for purposeful action.* Whether you sell furniture, build or fly jets, create software, teach, conduct research, grow or process food, treat animals, or serve in public office, your vision must be to serve others first. A written vision statement is the inspiration to drive an idea. It is different from a mission statement and goals. A vision statement is created and shared by members or clients within the organization to inspire their future efforts. The statement should be brief, simple, and above all else, inspiring. Hallmark's success is driven by a powerful yet simple vision: "when you care enough to send the very best." If love is missing in the vision statement, forget about success.

2. *Share your innermost thoughts about the values you hold and what your employees can expect from you.* Explain that you and all members of the organization will do the right things, use supportive communications, and work as teams to ensure top quality. Explain that mistakes will be made but that failure is not fatal. Thomas Edison's experiments to develop the light bulb failed many times. Undaunted by each failure, he merely chirped, "I have learned not to try that again." His last try on October 21, 1879, gave us electric lights. People who are loved and trusted will try new ideas and go the extra mile for you and the organization.

3. *Keep everyone informed about the entire organization—successes as well as failures.* Pay attention to detail by providing good data to all employees as a sign that you believe in their abilities to solve problems when and where they find them. Empowering all employees creates more power for you and the products or people you develop. Vision with love has the power to motivate the organization to change to meet the future and create productive teams that prize the diverse personalities and talents of every person.

Making It Work

A Proved Team Visioning Strategy. The following team visioning activity is a successful model in helping individual organizational members focus on the future. Rather than helping particpants look into the future, this exercise motivates participants to look back at their climb to success and reflect on steps the organization took on its road to outstanding success.

Title of Exercise: Tell the Good News Story. Your leadership team has just received word that your organization has been selected by the Baldrige Foundation, the Office of the President of the United States, and the U.S. Chamber of Commerce as America's most successful, innovative, and client-centered organization. Within the hour, the president, executives with the Baldrige Foundation, and the executive director of the chamber of commerce will arrive at your office with a CNN news team to ask you the following questions:

- What three steps did the leadership of your organization take in the last nine years to lead to this day of high honor?
- What three pieces of advice will you share with the visiting dignitaries and others throughout America viewing this newscast?

The Process. Conduct the activity by following these steps:

Step 1. Organize the leadership team into groups of no more than 10, and ask each group to select a facilitator. Identifying the person with the most recent birthday is a quick and fair way to determine the facilitator.

Step 2. The team facilitator will then repeat the challenge to select three steps taken during the past nine years that will be shared with the dignitaries and a national viewing audience.

Step 3. The facilitator will then give each member five minutes to write his or her three steps to success on a pad.

Step 4. Using a flip chart or white board, the facilitator records the ideas from each member (one idea each round) and continue until all steps/ideas are recorded and numbered.

Step 5. The facilitator asks each member to look over all recorded items and prepare to vote on each one.

Step 6. The facilitator asks all members to place their right elbows on the tabletop and prepare to vote on each item. An open hand (five fingers) is five points (five points may be used only twice), four fingers are four points, and so on.

Step 7. When the facilitator calls for item number one, each member will immediately vote with five, four, three, two, one, or no fingers (participants should be encouraged to vote without checking a neighbor's vote).

Step 8. The facilitator, with the assistance of another member, counts the total finger votes for each item and places the number after each item.

Step 9. The three steps/ideas with the highest total votes are the three steps that will be shared with the dignitaries and CNN. In case of a tie, the group may discuss the items and either combine them or include all four steps to share.

Visionary leadership is knowing how to inspire hearts, ignite minds, and move hands to create tomorrow.

—John R. Hoyle

3

Communicating With Love

Anything will give up secrets if you love it enough. Not only have I found that when I talk to the little flower or to the little peanut, they will give up their secrets, but I have found that when I silently commune with people, they give up their secrets also—if you love them enough.

—George Washington Carver,
quoted in Seymour, 1979, p. 53

Communication requires senders and receivers. Although this appears to be a simple connection, we as individuals know better. We try to communicate with others in loving, patient, and tolerant ways during stressful, disruptive times, but our primitive urges override our best intentions. The importance of communicating with love came home to a popular professor who had touched thousands of lives during her 31-year teaching career. She was diagnosed with cancer, and during her surgeries and long days in the hospital, she talked about how a nurse's remark or a doctor's sigh could give a patient hope or despair. "You depend on other people and how they talk to you—you feel like a puppet in a way. That just reiterated the point when you're working with a patient, you need to consider them as a person" (Clancy, 2001, p. D1).

We rush from task to task struggling to communicate and wonder why our words and gestures are not understood by others. The outpourings of words that blast us each day come in various tones and meanings and cause us to say and do unloving things at home and in the workplace.

According to futurist Richard Worzel, today's society is at the infancy of information overload. According to some estimates, the amount of information doubles each year, and in 15 years, there will be more than 1,000 bits of data for each fact in existence (Olofson, 2001). Reliable information is becoming more difficult to identify, but individuals who communicate the right information and use it for the common good will be the power brokers of this century. When a meeting or a project deadline is missed, we blame it on miscommunication or a failure to communicate. It could merely be a hearing problem similar to that of the older gentleman who told his good friend about his brand-new, superpowerful hearing aid. He said, "This new hearing aid is so powerful, I can hear cockroaches walking across my kitchen sink." His friend asked, "What kind is it?" "Three-thirty," he responded.

Good communication is hard work under the best of circumstances. Marriages, friendships, teams, corporations, and other organizations fall apart and battles are lost when communications fail. The case study at the end of this chapter is a challenge to consider alternative solutions to a destructive, loveless communication problem among members of an urban community college board of trustees.

Universities and corporations conduct research and spend millions preparing and developing executives to lead organizations. These executives learn financial marketing, accounting, systems, human motivation, the law, visioning and planning, and human relations. Love-based interpersonal communication, however, the most important skill other than business ethics, is stressed little, if at all.

Angeles Arrien (1998) found that "most fired executives are poor communicators" and that "it is safe to assume that the problems encountered at work are mostly communicative, not substantive" (p. 2). A construction manager told me about frustrations in training new employees to carry out their jobs at construction sites. He said, "I often run out of patience telling these young inexperienced people how to do the simplest jobs. I wind up telling some of them the same things several times—they just don't get it."

The director of a university development foundation got a phone call from a wealthy former student who had given sizable sums of money in past years. The former student told the director, "Bob, in the last 24 hours, I had two of your young development people call me to set up a luncheon to talk about two different 'opportunities' for me to contribute to your foundation. What gives here?" Bob apologized and told him that he would look into the situation and get back to him soon. Bob called in his two eager fundraisers and asked them why they both contacted the same person about contributions. One said, "I thought you told me to contact him." The other said, "That's strange, I could swear you told me to make the contact."

Did the teller or the listener fail to communicate? Bob reprimanded them with carefully selected words about their mistake and excused them from his office. After a quick perusal of the donor list, he found the source of the problem. Two donors shared the same last name and first initial, but only one was contacted. No big deal you say? The mistake may cost the university more than a million dollars!

This scenario is played out in hundreds of organizations each hour. Medical health teams that fail to communicate can cause mistakes during surgery and mix-ups in medications. Air disasters have resulted from confused traffic controller and pilot communications. Less serious communication mistakes happen daily at airport pickup points. The art and science of communication with love must be given serious attention by all executives if they are to lead successful organizations. Managers in all types of organizations spend 90% of the workday communicating. It is the most critical skill that we as leaders have in telling our stories and persuading people to share our visions for success.

The Art and Science of Communication

Professor Albert Meharbian (1971) of UCLA conducted the most startling research on the art and science of communication. Meharbian found that the visual impact of the presenter on the listener represents 55% of the total impact, vocal impact is 38%, and the actual words used have an impact of only 7%. On the basis of this research, if people are pleased with the speaker's appearance and overall presence and like the quality of his or her voice and personality, the speaker can communicate successfully with the group or audience although the words have only 7% impact. Communications specialist Bert Decker (1992) believes that Meharbian found the components needed to form a complete message that is believable and has impact (pp. 83-85).

Communication is far more than two or more persons trying to interpret each other's messages. The message must express love and be heard and understood by everyone in the organization. According to Goldhaber (1974), "Organizational communication is the flow of messages within the network of independent relationships." A few common strands vital to ensure the communication flow are as follows:

1. Organizational communication occurs within a complex open system that is influenced by and influences the environment.
2. Organizational communication involves messages, their flow, purpose, direction, and media.

3. Organizational communication involves people, their attitudes, feelings, relationships, and skills. (p. 11)

People seem to work at making organizational communications complex. We talk about keeping everyone informed and then shelter information that management deems confidential. How many times each week do we hear a colleague complain about not being told about a new project, job reassignments, or a staff meeting? The excuse for these communication foul-ups is often, "Don't you read your e-mail?" Bruce Tulgan (2000), the Studs Terkel for Generation X, tells us that Xers are more comfortable information processors than their baby boomer bosses. Xers thrive on e-mail, fax machines, voice mail, beepers, and cellular phones. Although these technologies dramatically increase the flow of information, they are not solving organizational communications problems. Xers, according to Tulgan,

are in a hurry to learn for good reason; in an era where technological change is a constant, there is a premium on quick mastery. What is more, the ability to cope with massive quantities of information quickly is sure to be the key survival skill of the 21st century work place. (p. 69)

Xers and their older managers must work to close the communication gaps among groups with different backgrounds. Accurate organizational communication depends primarily on management's taking time to visit with employees. People feel empowered when the boss drops by for a face-to-face chat about organizational successes and problems, rather than communicating in a faceless chat room. Workers in small organizations may be well informed about each job role and responsibility, whereas those in larger organizations rarely have the big picture about various roles and responsibilities.

Management guru Peter Drucker (1985) tells us that despite new information technologies, communication in larger organizations has improved little through the years. We have known since Chester Barnard's classic *Functions of the Executive* (1938/1968) that top-down communications are not conducive to peak performance (McGregor, 1964). This failure to reverse communication flow defies logic. Drucker (1985) reminds us that in successful knowledge organizations, "the effective work is actually done by teams of people of diverse knowledge and skills" (p. 66). The best strategy to inform all employees is to bring small groups together from different job areas in the organization. Large mass meetings designed to tell employees about job roles and department duties are not effective.

Visibility and Communication

Abby, a high school math teacher, recalls attending a required meeting at the beginning of the school year with hundreds of other teachers. After the session, Abby and her friends went to a local restaurant for a few drinks to gripe about the mass meeting. After a few cutting remarks and raucous laughter, a gentleman stepped over to the group and said, "Hey, not so loud, it doesn't reflect well on your employer." After he left, Abby asked, "Who was that man?" A woman at the next table responded, "Our school superintendent!" The math teachers gained little from the general session but a lot of embarrassment for not recognizing their boss. If this superintendent wants to change this perception, he must become visible on all campuses, in classrooms, and at sporting and other events. A key to communicating with love is being visible when people need you.

When employees understand the important contributions of their jobs to the overall success of the organization and can talk about it in small groups, they tend to respond to job training more willingly. As James Kouzes and Barry Posner (1993) write,

> Leaders understand that unless they communicate and share information with their constituents, few will take much interest in what is going on. Unless people see and experience the effects of what they do, they won't care. When people have the same information and understand that they are part of a community, with common values and shared interests, the results flow. (p. 172)

Managers who communicate with love to share information inspire employees to do their part in ensuring high quality.

The Communication Walls in Higher Education

Higher education institutions are notorious for poor communication across colleges and departments. These medieval organizational structures make it difficult for colleges and universities to be model learning organizations. Despite faculty senates, curriculum committees at the undergraduate and graduate levels, Web pages, and e-mail, rank-and-file professors have little notion of what is taught outside their field. For example, it is not unusual for several colleges or departments to offer courses in leadership and management using the same textbooks, for example, business management, public administration, educational administration, management of human resources, sports management, and agricultural administration. Despite the 75% overlap in course content, the professors rarely engage in conversation about their courses.

On rare occasions, an interdisciplinary team will create a curriculum for honors students; otherwise, the walls of colleges and departments are well guarded to avoid sharing student credit-hour money across campus. These communication barriers create problems for students in courses outside their majors.

Students frequently complain about professors who teach service courses to nonmajors. The professors complain that the students are not interested in their specialties and merely want to slide by for the three-hour credit, and the students feel that the professors make little effort to make the course content relevant to their majors. The teaching method in these service courses is usually traditional one-way lecture format with little or no class discussion, feedback, or team project work.

Laura and Amy, two future elementary school teachers, had vastly different experiences in separate math classes. Laura told a horror story about her professor with a foreign accent who told them the first day that he was not interested in helping the students learn how to teach math to children but that he would teach math and let them figure out how to teach it. Laura merely survived the class and learned little about math or how to teach it. Amy had a much better experience. Her Chinese professor was a little difficult to understand, but the professor told them the first day that she knew that many in the class planned to teach. She told them that she would make every effort to communicate the intricacies of mathematics and demonstrate the best methods to teach math to young students. Both professors had accents, but one took time to find out about the students' career goals, made the course relevant, and communicated with love for her subject and her students. The students' course evaluations of the two instructors were on the extreme ends of the scale.

Efforts are under way in many universities to encourage faculty and students to avail themselves of other areas of study by offering professional development in interdisciplinary teaching and in the use of the latest teaching technologies. Thus far, the obsolete organizational-structural barriers have restricted any significant cross-disciplinary developments in higher education throughout the country.

These barriers explain the less-than-warm reception of the total quality management (TQM) movement in the academic sector of higher education. The idea of continuous improvement teams and efforts to identify outcome measures of effectiveness work well in the maintenance and student affairs divisions, but attempts to bring professors from different disciplines together have been futile. Only under orders will university scholars give up time to support the administration's quest for quality improvement. One rebellious professor said it this way: "I spend long hours in my research, advising students, and teaching to improve quality. I certainly do not need to waste my valuable time in small groups chatting about quality assurance."

Egos seem to get in the way when people attempt to communicate with love about the importance of what they do and how well they claim to do it. As humans, we find it difficult to listen to others when we view them as a threat to our area of expertise and hold misperceptions about them and their knowledge.

The office of public information in a large southwestern university published a newsy *Fortnightly* for all faculty and staff that included announcements about coming events and listings of faculty honors, presentations, publications, and research grants. This informative publication could be perused in three minutes by busy faculty and staff to keep up with the activities of friends and colleagues across campus. In addition, it sparked numerous collaborative activities among faculty from different departments.

Five years ago, however, *Fortnightly* was dropped in favor of a Web page. With strong belief in the information gods, the public information department decided that "faculty can get information from our Web page if they really want it." Although most faculty are computer literate, hits on the Web page are now minimal. Faculty members complained that they enjoyed holding the publication in their hands, rather than turning on their computers, to read about the accomplishments of their friends. The Web has not replaced the value of the *Fortnightly*, and the communication walls have become higher. Where is the love in substituting Web technology for a print publication that had improved communication among more than 3,000 faculty and staff in a complex university?

Listening With Heart and Ears

A manager of a medium-sized men's clothing store asked a customer how things were going in his life. The customer responded, "Well, I just got over the flu, my dog died, my daughter flunked out of the university, and my sock has a hole in the heel." The store manager responded, "Good, what size and color sock do you want?" The manager forgot love in his communication, and the customer walked out of his store. Wendy Nomathemba Luhabe (1998) knows that persons will not listen to others unless they listen with their hearts and ears. She believes that "the way to our heart is through our ears. If someone says, 'I love you,' I hear that with my ears before my heart is invoked. Therefore, the ear is a vital communication bridge between people" (p. 76). Even when we listen with our heart and ears, however, our attention may not be returned. But if you communicate with love for others, Hogan (2000) believes that "you will gain from the love and integrity you share" (p. 33).

As Chapter 1 related earlier, Mitch Albom (1997) tells a powerful story in *Tuesdays With Morrie* about spending every Tuesday with his favorite professor, Morrie Schwartz, who was dying. Morrie liked for Mitch to call him "Coach." During Mitch's last visit with his critically ill friend, he asked, "Coach, I don't know how to say good-bye." Coach patted Mitch's hand and placed it on his chest. "This . . . is how we say . . . good-bye . . . love you," he rasped. "I love you, too, coach." "Know you do—know something else?—" "What else do you know?" "You always have." At Morrie's funeral, Mitch remembered Coach telling him, "You talk and I'll listen." Mitch writes, "I tried doing that in my head and to my happiness, found that the imagined conversation felt almost natural. I looked down at my hands, saw my watch, and realized why. It was Tuesday" (pp. 185-186).

We All Make Mistakes

Bad news must be accepted without shooting the messenger. The capacity to listen and have compassion for the bearer of bad news is a sign of leading with love. Typos can be corrected, reorders can be sent, reports can be amended, but angry words of reprimand cannot be changed. The Old Testament records that Samson the strong man killed 10,000 Philistines with the jawbone of an ass. Today, we create similar mayhem using the same weapon (Booher, 2000).

The ability to listen to bad news and respond with calm, thoughtful reactions is remembered by employees much longer than the mistake they made. On her first day on the job, a secretary made two clerical errors. Fearing a reprimand, she approached her new boss to ask forgiveness for the errors. The supervisor looked up into the repentant eyes of the secretary and reached into her desk for a pencil. She said, "This pencil has two ends, one for writing and one for erasing mistakes. Mistakes are part of the job; erase them and move on." This is communicating with love.

The Power of Persuasive Communication

Without the gift of persuasion, managers cannot sell a vision to others in the organization. According to management scholars George Manners and Joseph Steger (1979), persuasion is difficult to teach and learn. Of the nine leadership and management skills they identify, persuasion is the most difficult to master. This explains the shortage of great salespersons in all occupations.

The art of persuasive communication enables the leader to get people to do things contrary to their own wishes and desires. Managers must convince others—often those over whom they have no administrative control—to follow them in a project or idea. When speaking to individuals, groups, or large gatherings, managers must get them personally involved by touching their emotions about their work, family, or personal ambitions. To persuade others, leaders must express love and be sincere, enthusiastic, and honest in their remarks. Leaders must touch the audience's hearts to turn their heads.

Great leaders are remembered for their vision and ability to spark others through the art of persuasion to join in creating the vision and seeking excellence. On December 22, 1944, at Bastogne, during the Battle of the Bulge, General Anthony McAuliffe used only one word to persuade his troops. Surrounded by a German Panzer division, a German messenger handed McAuliffe a note from General Fritz Bayerlein telling him to surrender or be killed. The messenger returned to General Bayerlein with a response from McAuliffe that simply read, "Nuts." This act of defiance and love in the face of danger rallied McAuliffe's men to break out of the enemy trap and turn the tide of the battle (Ambrose, 1997).

Clear, simple persuasive communication with love can move others to great accomplishments. Persuasion has taken on new meanings in the age of cultural diversity. As time passes, whites, blacks, Hispanics, Asian Americans, men, and women are engaged in face-to-face discussions each hour of the day. We find less difficulty persuading those who share common traits, such as gender, race, religious and political beliefs, accents, and education levels.

Until recently, according to John and Catherine Kikoski (1996),

America's organizations had one dominant culture with an accompanying single order of talk—white, Anglo-Saxon, Protestant male. Demographically, tomorrow's world will be even more different. . . . The more we get to know who we are as individuals, the less stereotyping we engage in and the more we treat each other equally and respect-fully. (p. 15)

Persuading others from different cultures and experiences to share a vision is complex. Scott Cutlip, Allen Center, and Glen Broom (1985), spe-cialists in public relations and the art of persuasion, offer four guiding principles to help managers lead diverse groups:

1. Identification Principle. Most people will ignore an idea or point of view unless they see that it affects their personal fears, desires, hopes, and aspirations.
2. Action Principle. People seldom buy ideas separated from ac-tion—either action taken by the sponsor of the idea or action that the people themselves can conveniently take to prove the merit of the idea.
3. Principle of Familiarity and Trust. We buy ideas only from those we trust; we are influenced by, or adopt, only those opinions or points of view put forward by individuals, corporations, or insti-tutions that we regard as credible.
4. Clarity Principle. The situation must be clear to us, not confusing. To communicate, one must employ words, symbols, or stereo-types that the receiver comprehends and responds to. (pp. 178-179)

In the world of overchoice and info-flooding, managers must express love to touch the hearts of employees, provide the resources and dem-onstrate how to get a job done, establish trust, and clearly communicate each step toward goal accomplishment. Too much trust, however, be-came a problem for my cousin Elmer. Blind trust and loyalty can be the downfall of people and organizations.

One warm summer day in 1943 in Chickasha, Oklahoma, my cousin Elmer and I were pretending to be comic book heroes Captain Marvel and Superman by wearing capes made from Mother's old red curtains. We ran around the yard "plikin" (playing like) we were saving the world from the evil deeds of robbers and other criminal sorts. During our dar-ing deeds, Elmer said to me, "I wish I could really fly like Superman." Now, you must understand that I was seven, one year older, and much taller than Elmer, and he would do anything I told him. I replied, "You can fly, Elmer—just climb up on the garage and take a running leap into the air." Elmer quickly climbed on top of the garage, held up his cape, and began his run and dive screaming "Superman!" Elmer hit the grass with a loud thud but no crying because the impact left him breathless. I ran into the house and told Aunt Elizabeth that Elmer was hurt. She ran to Elmer's side and began pumping air into his chest. Elmer turned his skinned face toward me and, with grass and dirt in his mouth, asked weakly, "John, did I fly?" I responded, "Yes, for a little while."

At a family gathering years later, Elmer walked up to me and asked, "John, why did you make me jump off your garage?" After all those years, I had no answer for him, but it was clear that Elmer has never forgotten blindly following his leader. The lesson learned is never to blindly follow a persuasive person regardless of how good the landing appears to be.

Love for others is the most persuasive force to urge us to learn more about the culture, communication patterns, and talents of our colleagues. To become effective leaders, Xers and others frozen to the Web, chat rooms, and e-mail must step away from the computers and interact as warm, caring, and talented individuals. More information is not the answer to higher performance, but information carefully scanned by executives to help them understand diverse workplaces and a powerful communicator with a servant's heart can persuade others to perform miracles.

Fired School Superintendents and Poor Communications

Central to understanding and managing conflict is the ability of the school superintendent to communicate effectively with his or her school board members. Members of school boards are elected either because voters view them as community leaders who want the best education for all students or because a segment of the community has a special ax to grind and wants to elect its advocate. These lay leaders are not educated in the finer points of educational management but must hire professionally educated superintendents who have the communication skills to lead the board and the school district. For many reasons, however, the communications between board members and superintendents can go sour. "Poor communication" has become the code for a wide range of negative factors in board-superintendent relations.

Superintendents who fail to communicate adequately with the board, either by commission or omission, create hidden agendas that lead to mistrust, suspicion, excessive conflict, and micromanagement by board members. Communication misfires produce unmanageable conflict, lead to poor school leadership, and ultimately create personal disaster at evaluation time for the superintendent. When a superintendent's contract is not renewed, the news release rarely states that the superintendent lacked leadership, curriculum, or technology skills. The most common reason given by the board to the press after a nonrenewal of a superintendent's contract is "differences between the board and the superintendent over the direction of the district."

The superintendent may hold a Ph.D. degree, develop beautiful strategic plans for the district, present high test scores to the media, and have strong rapport with the business community, but if the superintendent is noncommunicative with the teaching staff, parents, and school board, his or her days are numbered. Differences between the board and superintendent over the direction of the district is another way of saying "poor communications" (Hoyle & Skrla, 1999, pp. 407-408). When love is missing, communication has little impact on inspiring staff to work together and solve problems in all types of organizations.

A Football Coach's Failure to Communicate

Why would a winning football coach of a major university resign his position at midseason? A failure to communicate is the only answer. This well-known and respected coach had coached state champions in high school and had a reputation as a university assistant coach with offensive genius. When he was hired by the board of regents to turn the football program around, he responded with six winning seasons and defeated the in-state archrival two times but had failed to win a conference championship. These winning years led to better recruiting, touchdown club donations reached an all-time high, and current and former students held their heads high with pride because the team was no longer last in the league. To start the seventh season, the director of athletics, the athletics council, the board of regents, and fans around the world were looking forward to a conference title and a chance to play for the national championship. Area media selected the team to win the title and wind up in the nation's Top 10.

During the third season of the coach's tenure, a new university president was appointed. The new president was mildly interested in football and made few efforts to talk with the coach about the team or the coming season. The coach viewed the president as an "unfriendly academic type" and made little effort to communicate with him. Although a communication barrier existed between the two strong personalities, there was little cause for the coach to be concerned because the team was winning and the president had other issues more important than football to deal with.

The seventh season began with a less-than-convincing victory over a small institution from Louisiana, followed by three close calls against weaker conference foes. Although former students were griping about the mediocre play of the team, at least the team was winning. Then a stunning loss to a two-wins, three-losses conference team made the wolves howl, but the coach reasoned that a victory in the next game against the University of Arkansas would heal all wounds and silence most of his critics. Because his team had superior athletes and the home field advantage, the victory seemed within reach. His team took the field in front of 76,000 hopeful fans, and when the game ended, the scoreboard read Arkansas 31-0. The home fans yelled at the team and coach, the athletic director was flooded with irate phone calls and e-mails, and the news media had a field day with the inept performance of the home team.

One radio sports announcer issued an anonymous report that the former students were planning to buy up the coach's contract and that the president and the board of regents were holding a Sunday afternoon meeting. After the embarrassing loss and hearing the news stories about his demise, the coach called a loyal friend in the athletic department about the rumors. The longtime friend told the coach that he had heard that the president had called a news conference for 10:00 a.m. Monday morning to announce the coach's firing.

Late that Sunday evening, the coach called the president and requested a meeting at 7:30 a.m. on Monday morning in the president's office. The next morning, without saying a word, the coach handed the president his letter of resignation. After reading the letter, the president looked up at the angry coach and said, "Why did you write this?" The coach responded, "Well, I have never been fired from a job, and I didn't want to start now." After a brief pause, the president said, "I accept this resignation with regret, since you have brought a winning record to our university and I anticipated your leadership to continue for several more years." The comment caught the coach by surprise, and he asked, "You mean you were not going to fire me this morning?" "Fire you? Where did you get that crazy idea?" "Well, the news conference—what was it for?" asked the coach. With a look of puzzlement, the president said, "The news conference was to announce a two-million-dollar contribution to the College of Agriculture."

The news media found out about the resignation letter by 9:00 a.m., and at 10:00 a.m., the president announced the large donation and called another news conference at 3:00 p.m. to announce the coach's resignation. This story about a noncommunicative football coach and university president is no different from hundreds of other organizations in which communication is treated like a bad four-letter word. According to John and Catherine Kikoski (1996), communication disasters are all too common. They remind the reader about the frequent refrain, " 'But I thought I told you to—' followed by, 'But I thought you said that—' " (p. 16). When trust and love guide communication between two highly competitive individuals, considerable time, money, and face can be saved.

The Megalopolis Communications Mess: A Case Study

The following case study is an example of what can happen when people fail to communicate because ego, anger, and disappointment force love and human understanding out of the process.

You are an experienced CEO and consultant hired by Megalopolis Community College District as a human relations-communications consultant to help resolve a contentious situation among members of the college system trustees and the chancellor of the system. Your consulting contract includes a generous honorarium, two staff assistants, and all travel and other expenses. You have taken two days out of your demanding schedule to meet with the principals in the community college district before agreeing to take the job. You gathered the following detailed information about the history of the situation, the key people, and several stormy meetings during the past two years.

The Megalopolis Community College District board of trustees consists of five white and four minority members elected by geographical districts. The tax-supported system enrolls more than 40,000 students who receive two-year degrees or credentials in a wide variety of career preparation programs. Although the district has a good reputation for providing educational opportunities to urban and suburban students, the trustees are in constant conflict with each other and the administration.

During the past two years, the trustees recruited a highly respected urban community college president from the Northeast to assume the role of president at Megalopolis. Within six months, the president's plans for improvement and change met with resentment by various board members who charged the president with poor communications and favoritism to women in administrative positions and budget recommendations.

After several bitter confrontations between the president and board members, the president announced her resignation, citing excessive micromanagement and unprofessional and abusive behavior by certain board members. This resignation, caused by the communications nightmare, was followed by a visiting team from a national accrediting agency. Its report criticized the trustees and recommended major steps to improve communications and interpersonal relationships among board members and chief administrators.

As a result of the report, two nationally known authorities on conflict resolution and organizational communications were hired by the board trustees to help ease the problem by building bridges across the vast chasms of difference. The consultants began interviewing all parties in the conflict and, in the process, uncovered a key problem that created racial politics among the board. The consultants found that the white members of the board had been negotiating to annex a large public school district that was 70% white.

When the annexation proposal came to the board, the four minority trustees voted against the annexation, claiming that it would violate the law and be detrimental to minority students living in other areas of Megalopolis. This negative vote created the appearance of a racial standoff, with the new president and staff caught in between.

Six sessions to resolve the conflict led to more verbal confrontation in which no one was listening and each was trying to outshout the others. During the sixth session, after the consultants managed to take control of another verbal storm, they recommended that the trustees needed to listen and be courteous to each other if they were ever going to be able to work together to build a better system for the students in Megalopolis.

The chairman of the board then called for a closed session to consider the consultants' recommendations and discuss their differences. After an hour attempting to discuss their differences of opinion, they were still divided on several issues along racial and geographic lines. They then decided that to resolve the stalemate, they needed an experienced leader with a successful track record in managing an organization to help them take the next steps. They made a list of possible consultants, and your name came to the top. You accepted the contract to help the trustees and administrators overcome their communications problems and work together for the welfare of the college system.

Solution: What steps will you take to meet this challenge? What can you do to turn the communications from disdain to love?

A great class or executive training activity for this case is to divide participants into groups of 12 and assign roles to each member. Place fictitious names in a hat at each table and ask participants to draw their assignments. The assignments include four minority and five Anglo trustees, the board chair (minority), a college president, vice president for operations, and you, the consultant. The chair of the trustees begins the meeting by introducing each person and then turns the meeting over to the president, who makes a few remarks before introducing you, the consultant. Good luck!

> *So long as we love, we serve; so long as we are loved by others, I would almost say that we are indispensable; and no man is useless while he has a friend.*
>
> —Robert Louis Stevenson,
> quoted in Seymour, 1979, p. 5

4

Teamworking With Love

It's the only game you'll watch all year where eighteen guys will be on the ground after the opening kickoff.

—Dick Vermeil, pregame comment, Army-Navy
1995, quoted in Feinstein, 1996, p. 343

Author John Feinstein calls the annual Army-Navy football game a civil war. Army coach Bob Sutton said it best: "The most desperate team wins Army-Navy games" (Feinstein, 1996, p. 146). The recipe for any winning team must go beyond desperation to become a blend of individual skills, clear focus, selfless performance, and a dash of persistence molded by love.

Management expert Peter Drucker understands Vermeil's comment about team dedication and organizational success. Drucker predicts that organizations of the future will succeed only if players share the passion to achieve a common goal. Drucker (1994) emphasizes the importance in the knowledge society of teams working to improve organizations.

Recruiters for business, medical professions, the military, education, law enforcement, and government are looking for self-motivated team players who value collaboration. World-renowned symphonies are admired not merely for their first violinists but for the entire ensemble. Orchestras do not succeed on the basis of competition among the sections; they succeed through collaboration and a conductor who has the skill to blend talent and timing into harmony. Before continuing, ask yourself if you are a team player. Perhaps the checklist in Box 4.1 will provide some insight into your success or failure as a worthy teammate.

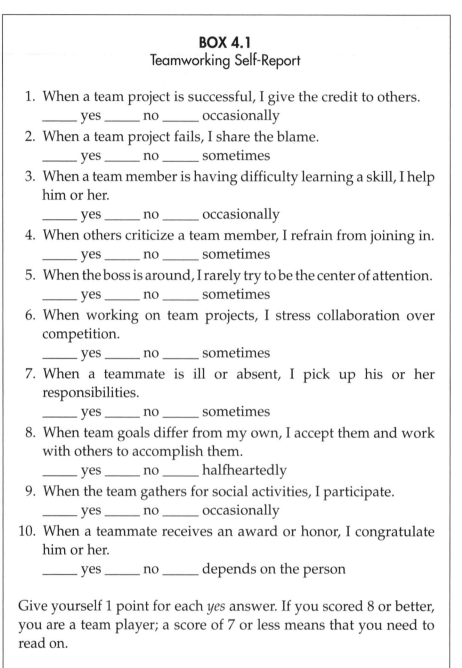

BOX 4.1
Teamworking Self-Report

1. When a team project is successful, I give the credit to others.
   _____ yes _____ no _____ occasionally

2. When a team project fails, I share the blame.
   _____ yes _____ no _____ sometimes

3. When a team member is having difficulty learning a skill, I help him or her.
   _____ yes _____ no _____ occasionally

4. When others criticize a team member, I refrain from joining in.
   _____ yes _____ no _____ sometimes

5. When the boss is around, I rarely try to be the center of attention.
   _____ yes _____ no _____ sometimes

6. When working on team projects, I stress collaboration over competition.
   _____ yes _____ no _____ sometimes

7. When a teammate is ill or absent, I pick up his or her responsibilities.
   _____ yes _____ no _____ sometimes

8. When team goals differ from my own, I accept them and work with others to accomplish them.
   _____ yes _____ no _____ halfheartedly

9. When the team gathers for social activities, I participate.
   _____ yes _____ no _____ occasionally

10. When a teammate receives an award or honor, I congratulate him or her.
    _____ yes _____ no _____ depends on the person

Give yourself 1 point for each *yes* answer. If you scored 8 or better, you are a team player; a score of 7 or less means that you need to read on.

Competitive Team Players

Great teams in industry, athletics, and music must have competitive players to reach the top of their fields. Championship basketball teams must have competitive players who excel in scoring points, passing, re-bounding, and setting screens. Each team member, however, must be un-selfish in carrying out a key role to strengthen team unity. Whether the team is a family, police investigators, school faculty, or a fast-food work group, combining role players' talents leads to success. Wal-Mart em-ployees are encouraged to compete with other discount stores but view themselves as members of the Wal-Mart family around the world. This family vision of service drives each employee to serve customers better than do the competitors.

Organizations that are tightly controlled by rules and policies are not conducive to effective teamwork. When the communication pattern is top to bottom and ruled by the chain of command, teams become guided missiles for management. These missiles are told when to fire, how to fly, and where to strike. If the team missiles hit the wrong target, manage-ment blames the teams for the failures.

Creativity and divergent thinking by employees are frowned on be-cause they must follow the strategic plan to the letter. When teamwork is encouraged, shared visions are pursued in an environment of greater freedom to create and of lessened fear of making mistakes.

The values of friendship, risk, trust, integrity, fun, and love are the hallmarks of successful team-based organizations. General Electric's for-mer CEO Jack Welch organized *boundarylessness* sessions to build the GE competitive team. Welch spoke metaphorically of a house when talking about removing barriers in the workplace.

- The *horizontal* barriers are the walls—such as functional units and geographic locations—that divide groups of peers into isolated compartments.
- The *vertical* barriers are the floors and ceilings that demarcate hierarchy. Organizations do need some layers, but when differ-ences in rank block open communications, hierarchy becomes self-defeating.
- The *external* barriers are the outside walls of the company. Beyond these walls are many groups with whom close working relation-ships are essential, such as customers, suppliers, and venture part-ners. (Tichy & Sherman, 1993, pp. 234-235)

In addition to the importance of removing the three barriers, the founda-tion of the house must rest on a solid base of caring and love for each other. Otherwise, the entire structure will soon tumble under its own bu-reaucratic weight.

Praise, Don't Blame

The key for any team leader—sales manager, school superintendent, hospital administrator, or coach—is to find out what each team member does best and enjoys doing and to provide the best possible training to help ensure high-performing teams. Team building is a never-ending process. Former Miami Dolphins coach Don Shula said it this way: "Success isn't forever, and failure isn't fatal." Shula's winning strategy was to identify each player's strengths, build on them, and encourage players to bounce back after a loss. It should come as no surprise that team members are more satisfied and perform at a higher level when they have a clear understanding of their job roles and are given proper training.

Management writers Marcus Buckingham and Donald Clifton's (2001) book, *Now, Discover Your Strengths,* details the value of strength-based training to improve employee performance in organizations. They report research by the Gallup organization that asked 198,000 employees in 7,939 business units in 36 companies the following question: "Do I have the opportunity to do what I do best every day?" Gallup data revealed that if the employees "strongly agreed" to the question, they were 50% more likely to work in organizations with lower employee turnover, 38% more likely to be in higher-performing teams or units, and 44% more likely to work in teams with superior customer satisfaction scores (p. 5).

We all like to display our best talents and be recognized for our successes. Reviewer Mark Henricks (2001) summed up Buckingham and Clifton's strength-based training: "We'll all do better if we concentrate on getting better at what we are really good at, rather than trying to do something we stink at" (p. 105).

The ghosts of 19th-century scientific management still hover over the workplace, veiled in criticism and faultfinding rather than in praise and helping employees succeed. Although research findings linking happy workers to higher productivity are inconclusive, the evidence indicates that workers engaged in tasks at which they succeed appear to be better adjusted and produce superior work. Michele Australie, who has trained 250 managers at the St. Paul Companies Inc. with strength-based strategies, is optimistic. She has seen a new enthusiasm among employees and predicts positive bottom-line success in her company (Henricks, 2001, p. 109).

Productive teams consist of individuals who love what they do and help each other excel in their roles. The greatest motivators are job achievement, the work itself, and positive recognition from team members and supervisors. An occasional "atta boy" or "atta girl" does wonders for strengthening bonds among individuals and turns a group into a team. Some job tasks are more pleasant than others, but when teams work together with enthusiasm for quality and meeting customer needs, the job becomes more enjoyable. Others hold jobs that they enjoy every day and are not concerned when observers call them workaholics. According to Douglas McGregor's (1964) Theory Y, work can be as enjoyable as play if individuals are free to use their best skills and are committed to the organization's objectives and to the welfare of others on the team.

Multimillionaire investor Warren Buffett told a group of future business leaders, "If there is any difference between you and me it may simply be that I get up every day and have a chance to do what I love to do, every day. If you want to learn anything from me, this is the best advice I can give you" (Buckingham & Clifton, 2001, p. 19).

People who love what they do live to work, rather than work to live. Most of my friends my age are retired and seem to be happy and find plenty to occupy their time. I find too much enjoyment in teaching and advising students and sharing ideas with colleagues at the university and around the world to call it quits. The joy in seeing students develop greater self-confidence and become successful professionals eases the headaches of the job. Although some faculty meetings could be better handled with e-mail, other meetings that focus on program improvement for the students tie faculty together and bring out creative ideas and solutions.

Occasional battles with doctoral committee members about the quality of a dissertation sometimes make me question my sanity for not following my colleagues into quieter pastures. But any job comes with unpleasant "opportunities" and petty politics that cause anxious moments. These issues need not detract from the work enjoyed, the achievements recorded, and the recognition received for a job well done.

Teams in any organization with individuals who are enthusiastic about their jobs elicit a magnetism for each other and for successfully completing each assignment. Author and psychologist Wayne Dyer (1998) advises us to "know in your heart that doing what you love, and loving what you do, is far superior to loving what you may produce or the compensation you receive for your labor" (p. 199).

This love for work can be contagious to colleagues who have lost the love for their work somewhere along life's pathway. Team members who love what they do and help others excel at what they love create a culture of commitment and caring for quality outcomes and for each team member.

A popular movie, *Office Space*, provides numerous examples of ways to destroy teams through constant hassles, meaningless job expectations, and criticism. Peter, the main character, is a computer software technician who finds himself in a boss-led company that is concerned about point-less memos, especially about a new cover sheet for company TPS reports, rather than allowing him to do what he does best. Within one hour, three of Peter's eight bosses chastise him for not including a cover sheet on his TPS report.

The final straw comes when the boss tells Peter, "I'm going to need you to come in on Saturdays and Sundays, and since we lost some people, we need to play catch up." The negative tone of this movie was intended to spoof the cubicle work world, but the humor is lost in the realities of modern corporate life.

When teamwork is driven by competition rather than collaboration, individuals become noncommunicative and combative, and little nur-turing or love remains. Competition was the management strategy of a corrugated box company in Sand Springs, Oklahoma, until trouble among workers began. Management rewarded machine operators on the basis of the number of boxes they produced each eight-hour shift. Some machinists were faster than others, which was evident in the weekly pay checks. C.D., the most productive machinist during a five-year period, was selected by management to become a new line manager to oversee daily box production by each machinist.

After each shift, C.D. would collect a box count from each machinist to complete his report. Because the count was based on honesty, C.D. never questioned the machinists' word for several weeks until his obser-vations made him question the number counts. Each time that he asked several of the machinists where he could go and count their boxes, they would tell C.D., "The boxes have been loaded by my assistant in the box-cars outside." When C.D. matched the reported number with the actual number stacked in the boxcars, he found several discrepancies. C.D. con-fronted his machinists about their miscounts, who denied it and blamed C.D. for the mistakes.

Continued dishonest actions by some of the machinists led C.D. to in-form upper management. Within 24 hours, representatives of the ma-chinist union threatened C.D. with violence for blowing the whistle on some of their members. Management supported C.D. and leveled charges against some of the machinists, who were placed on probation. C.D. had been good friends with the machinists, but he became their en-emy and was told to watch his back.

The next year, the Sand Springs plant was bought by an international paper company that brought in management that stressed team collabo-ration, rather than competition. The new managers implemented contin-uous improvement and teamwork to replace competitive piecework.

Within six months, plant workers produced greater numbers of boxes with fewer errors. Dishonest behavior dissolved in favor of trust, teamwork, and customer satisfaction. C.D. was promoted to a management position. When he retired, he reflected on the power of trust and love in collaboration over mistrust and animosity growing from unhealthy competition.

Professors David Bradford and Allan Cohen (1984) provide insight into mature, shared-responsibility teams. They suggest the following guidelines for developing productive teams:

- Everyone knows his or her own and others' tasks well enough so that nothing falls through the cracks; everyone knows who is and who should be doing what.
- Trust is so high that the group does not need to meet on every issue because all members know and are committed to the same overarching goal and know each other's attitudes and positions on issues.
- Members who are clearly more expert than the others in certain areas are given greater latitude to make decisions on those matters.
- Although skilled at persuasion and willing to fight hard over important differences, members feel no obligation to automatically oppose initiatives from other members or the manager.
- The group pays attention to successful task achievement and to the individual member's learning.
- Perhaps most important, the group has self-correcting mechanisms; when things aren't going well, all members are ready to examine the group's processes, discuss what is wrong, and take corrective action. (pp. 174-175)

These six attributes of mature teams are found in the box factory in Sand Springs, the Ford Motor Company, Hallmark, and other successful organizations around the world. When management is reluctant to turn the organization over to teams, the organization will not become a player in the marketplace.

Some managers believe that group process and team structure result in "pooled ignorance" and lower productivity, with more kings than serfs. Thus, competition among employees is valued over team unity and collaboration. Although all successful organizations must have strong leaders who inspire, organize for action, and provide resources to make visions happen, collaboration dominates in successful organizational culture.

Leadership must be delegated and nourished in each employee to ensure that everyone is informed about what to do, how to do it, when to do it, and how to respect diversity in team members to seek quality in each task and final product. This collaborative process brings a family atmosphere to the workplace and creates respect for contributions by each member. Benjamin Canada (2000), past president of the American Association of School Administrators and superintendent of the Portland, Oregon, schools, shares three keys to team building and collaborative leadership:

No. 1. Know who your team is and what they do.
No. 2. Listen and hear what your team is saying.
No. 3. Expand your definition of team by involving your supporters and your critics. (p. 56)

The Xer generation believes in the team concept, provided that they have the support and opportunities from upper management to contribute to and influence team outcomes. Xer Bruce Tulgan (2000), who explores the working lives of persons born after 1963, writes, "We will express our commitments to the team by trying ever harder to improve and expand our own individual contributions, and we will be glad to do so in pursuit of shared team goals" (p. 201).

Violence at Work and School

Violence in the workplace and the schoolhouse has increased dramatically in recent years. The reasons for the increase are as complex as the deranged persons who carry out vendettas against selected individuals and random bystanders. One cause for such acts is often attributed to a feeling by the perpetrators that no person in the organization cares enough about them as individuals to spend time with them and help them feel wanted and respected. The two students at Columbine High School in Littleton, Colorado, who killed classmates, a teacher, and themselves were viewed by classmates as loners.

The 15-year-old boy who shot and killed two classmates at Santana High School in a suburb of San Diego, California, told others he was tired of being picked on by the popular kids. The same reasons were given by postal, factory, and corporate workers who killed people in a rage of revenge for being mistreated by coworkers. Psychologists and other experts have provided numerous reasons why individuals commit acts of violence at work or school.

A feeling of being ignored, laughed at, or constantly hassled by others on the job or at school is usually the first reason offered for individuals who commit violent acts against others. Corporations, agencies, and schools may have had preventive programs in place before the incidents but failed to identify the warning signs and find help for troubled individuals. The Care Club in Lenoir City (Tennessee) High School initiated by Coach Dave Moore is a model to help make kids who are different feel loved and respected. The Care Club is based on collaboration and inclusion, rather than competition and exclusion. Freaks, jocks, geeks, and rednecks are no longer isolated groups in Lenoir City. Coach Dave Moore, his colleagues, and parents know that love and respect for all students end cliques and competition and will reduce hatred and acts of violence.

Dave Moore told me that "the application of unconditional love for all students, teachers, and their families has been powerful in building a community that cares." All organizations could learn from the Lenoir City High School plan. When people know how much others care for them, there is little reason to want revenge or to commit acts of violence.

Managers in corporations, agencies, and education who know the value of collaboration and the impact of unconditional love for each person promote a family environment and the team concept. If people are given positive recognition and made to feel important in the organization, they will commit to organizational goals and to others in the organization. As Chapter 1 indicated, Robert Greenleaf (1991), an authority on servant leadership, reminds us that love and liability for others keep organizations strong.

The best way to express love and unlimited liability is by establishing teams of people who encourage each other and by helping them find fulfillment. Team-based organizations may not eliminate all acts of violence, but they will improve morale, strengthen friendships, reduce absenteeism, and lead to higher productivity.

The Case of the Barbie Doll Drill Team

The following case study is offered to create a lively discussion in a classroom or management development seminar. Divide the class into groups of six and allow approximately 10 minutes to read the case study. Next, ask each group to select a spokesperson (the person with the nearest birth date will work) and present a solution to the problems with the Barbie Doll Drill Team. Also, assign roles to individuals by drawing names or assignments.

Sarah Green, a management consultant, has been hired by Wayne Webster, superintendent of the Emerald Woods Independent School District, to help solve a major problem. The problem concerns the Emerald Woods award-winning girls' drill team. The drill team director,

Prissy Parton, a native of Emerald Woods and former captain of the drill team, is well-known in the community. After attending the state university, Prissy came home as a teacher and assistant drill team director. Two years later, she was named director. Prissy followed selection guidelines under which she and other girls in previous years had been selected for the drill team. Each year, girls were invited to try out before a panel of judges from the high school faculty. The drill team consisted of 40 girls in a high school with 2,500 students and an ethnic distribution of 51% white, 28% Hispanic, 14% black, and 7% Asian. Because Emerald Woods had been 85% white 10 years earlier, the demographic changes have been a challenge for the district and the community in cultural and educational diversity issues.

At the beginning of the spring semester, all girls in the school were invited to try out for the drill team. Of the 40 girls on the drill team, 20 would graduate in the spring, leaving 20 spots for new members. On the afternoon of the first tryouts, Prissy gathered her panel to discuss selection guidelines. Prissy told them that the girls to be selected should be no taller than 5'6", weigh no more than 130 pounds, and have good coordination. Each of the 65 girls competing for spots were asked to prepare a dance routine for one of three musical tapes selected by Prissy.

Of the 65 girls, only 30 met the Barbie Doll size and agility guidelines for selection. Of those 30, 25 were invited back for the final tryout, and 23 were selected to be members of the drill team for the coming year. Later that evening, Superintendent Webster received a call from an angry father about the drill team selection process. The father, Arturo Hernandez, told the superintendent that he came home to find his daughter crying her eyes out over her rejection by the drill team director, Prissy Parton.

After listening carefully to Mr. Hernandez's story, Webster tried to explain the exclusive selection process for drill team membership, but Hernandez did not accept the rationale. His little girl had been hurt by the process, and he wanted to know why such a thing could happen. In his eyes, she was the most beautiful, kind, and talented girl at Emerald Woods High School. He ended his conversation with Webster by saying,

> My daughter's best friend was the last pick, and my daughter and two others were told to try next year. I have talked to several other parents who want to know what kind of person would cut kids from a drill team based on physical size. They want to know why only two minorities made the cut. I am organizing a group of parents and community leaders to attend the next school board meeting, and we

want Prissy Parton to be present to answer our questions about her selection process.

The following Monday, the school board meeting room was standing room only. After a brief calm for immediate board actions, Mr. Hernandez was invited to make remarks to the board members. He directed his remarks to the board and to Prissy Parton. His voice was shaking in anger, and his remarks were met with cheers from the packed room. Hernandez protested vehemently that he would call in League of United Latin American Citizens (LULAC) lawyers and other influential people to get to the bottom of this racist, hurtful drill team selection process. At this point, the board chair, Bobbie Benson, declared the meeting adjourned. Later that evening, Wayne Webster called his school attorney about the situation. The attorney, Shirley Grissom, told him that this is an internal human relations problem that he must try to solve before seeking legal help.

Wayne got little sleep that night trying to decide his course of action. Early the next morning, he thought of Sarah Green, a specialist in team building and conflict resolution. She had a track record in helping a variety of organizations resolve difficult problems. Wayne placed a call to Green.

What steps should Sarah Green take to reach a solution to this serious issue?

> *As change agents, we have a responsibility to actively look for opportunities to cause people to come together. The worksite is an obvious avenue for building bridges as are schools and coalitions of religious organizations.*
>
> —Gary W. Janka, 1998, p. 53

5

Empowering With Love

The powerless live in a different world. Lacking the supplies, information, or support to make things happen easily, they may turn instead to the ultimate weapon of those who lack productive power—oppressive power: holding others back and punishing with whatever threats they can muster.

—Rosabeth Kanter, 1979, p. 67

In the first century A.D., Roman philosopher Lucius Annaeus Seneca understood the true meaning of power with these words: "Most powerful is he who has himself in his power." More than two thousand years later, Rosabeth Kanter, an authority on corporate power, understands that the more power one shares, the more power one gains. Thus these two prominent scholars, separated by time, share the belief that power must be respected, understood, and applied wisely if nations or organizations are to remain strong. The common definition of *power* is forcing people to do what you want them to do. *Power* and *force* have been synonyms in the lexicon of kings, queens, military leaders, dictators, and corporate and political leaders.

Joseph Stalin in the Soviet Union, Slobodan Milosevic in the former Yugoslavia, and Saddam Hussein in Iraq have used power to protect their position, wealth, and control of government. Misused power caused the birth of labor unions during the industrial revolution when immigrants and others desperate for jobs were forced to work long hours under dangerous conditions for low wages and no job benefits. Labor leader John L. Lewis and others successfully challenged the giant steel and automobile industries owned by millionaires such as Andrew Carnegie, John D. Rockefeller, and Henry Ford by means of crippling sit-down strikes. The union tactics created violent confrontations between strikers and corporate strikebreakers that led to legislation to protect the interests of both labor and management.

The U.S. Department of Labor, established in 1913, was followed by the Railway Labor Act, the National Labor Relations Board, and the Taft-Hartley Act. In the 1960s, César Chávez helped form the United Farm Workers Organizing Committee to fight the exploitation of farmworkers and led a nationwide boycott of California grapes to achieve labor contracts for his people.

History has a long, inglorious record of human misery caused by rulers of nations and magnates of big business. The French, American, and Russian revolutions were reactions by powerless people to overthrow ruthless and powerful rulers. Soviet dissident and writer Aleksandr Solzhenitsyn said it best: "Once you have stolen everything from the people, they are no longer under your power." When people feel powerless and have nothing to lose, they do desperate things.

Niccolò Machiavelli, a political writer in the early 1500s, advised Italian rulers to take the measures necessary to hold power over their subjects. Rulers may have to lie, cheat, or steal to maintain power, but they must always appear to be kind and good men. He advised them to inflict injury to the enemy quickly and to slowly gain their confidence by doling out rewards to their subjects while appearing to govern fairly.

Machiavelli's classic work, *The Prince* (1984), and other political treatises were the basis of a doctoral dissertation written by Italian dictator Benito Mussolini. Machiavelli's advice helped guide Mussolini's path to power with his fanatical speeches full of empty promises to the Italian people while giving the appearance of a caring, confident, skillful leader. His dreams of grandeur and thirst for power, however, led Italy to destruction and poverty. In disguise and hiding in a farmer's truck, Mussolini was caught attempting to escape over the Alps to Switzerland. His life and power were ended in 1945 by a bullet from his Italian underground captors, and his naked body was dragged through the streets and hung in Milan. If leaders hoard power and have a need to control others, they should never turn their backs.

Warfare genius Napoleon Bonaparte ruled with force, but late in his life, he discovered the real secret in power. He wrote, "Alexander, Caesar, Charlemagne, and I myself have founded empires; but upon what do these creations of our genius depend? Upon force. Jesus alone founded His empire upon love, and to this day millions would die for him" (Brownlow, 1972, p. 364).

Power Without Love

How many times have you felt powerless in your work situation? This feeling is not unusual in a world in which, according to Peter Block (1993),

> There is a dominant belief that leadership should come from the top and bosses are in some way responsible for their employees' performance and morale. . . . We have created a class system inside our institutions. There is a management class and an employee class. (p. 50)

The following scenario is familiar to many workers whose workforce has been downsized by the management class.

Executives of a medical records and equipment repair company made a business decision to fire 40 of 70 employees in a branch plant who had been with the company for 3 to 10 years. The hammer fell on the 40 employees when the corporate vice president flew in to deliver the fatal blow in a staff meeting. Jerry, the vice president, told the gathering,

> Our company has come on hard times caused by a market downtrend and by hospitals changing the way they handle medical records and repair their equipment. We regret to inform you that 40 of this workforce must be dismissed until financial times improve. You will find letters from my office in your boxes that explain your job future with our company. You have all been loyal, dedicated employees, and I wish those of you whom we must dismiss good luck in locating work. We will be happy to help you make contacts with similar companies in the nation and abroad and provide letters of reference.

The powerless looked at each other in nonbelief. One person said, "Is this a bad dream, or is what I just heard real?" Jerry closed his remarks with, "Well, I have a plane to catch; I'm sorry I have no time for questions." The 70 dazed employees rushed to the mail room to read their fate. The look on each face told the story as some gave a quiet sigh of relief, others broke into tears, and others audibly cursed the company and individual managers. None of the 40 dismissed had any advanced warning about their layoff. Moreover, to make things worse, medical benefits for all 70 employees had been canceled. One woman was expecting a baby soon, and two others had scheduled required surgery for the next week.

Why were these loyal employees not given at least two weeks' notice about their job status? Why were they not empowered by caring manage-

---

BOX 5.1

Powerless Times	*Powerful Times*
I had no input into a hiring decision of someone who was to report directly to me.	I was able to make a large financial decision on my own.
I worked extremely hard—long hours and late nights—on an urgent project, and then my manager took all the credit.	My president supported my idea without question.
My suggestions, whether good or bad, were either not solicited or—worse—ignored.	I wanted to put a new program into effect, but we'd reached the funding limit so my project was rejected. I went to a meeting with the president and asked him to take another look at the project. He did, turned to the VP, and said, "Fund it."

SOURCE: From Kouzes & Posner (1995, p. 183).

---

ment who provided counseling, job-finding advice, and medical benefits for an agreed-on time? Managers who use their power to control others and deny vital information to all employees create powerless people who will never share the organizational vision with management. Kouzes and Posner (1995) provide the following responses by people who have experienced "powerless times" and "powerful times" (Box 5.1).

Child advocate Marian Wright Edelman (1992), author of *The Measure of Our Success,* wrote a letter to her children and to everyone's children about the importance of feeling powerful for the right reasons. She warns them to "Never work just for money or for power. They won't save your soul or build a decent family or help you sleep at night" (p. 40).

From Power to Empowering With Love

The powerful who empower others become legends in any endeavor. Although power and force seem connected, empowerment and love are inextricably linked. To empower is to trust. Unconditional love and trust are synonymous. Peter Block (1993) defines empowerment as "the right to find purpose for ourselves" (p. 36). When we as leaders empower others, we believe that the people we trust will strive to act with integrity and in the best interest of the organization. Empowerment means a commitment to others in the workplace and to the customers who consume or use the product produced. Commitment is what I stress in conducting management training for supervisors in the red meat and poultry processing industry. Before each session, I display a visual labeled "generic citizen" and open with a plea to empower others in the slaughter and processing plants to commit to producing products that would not harm my six-year-old granddaughter, Jennifer.

My remarks to these veterinarians who hold stressful jobs are usually received well because they strive each day to meet industry standards. For them to add value beyond meeting the minimum standards, however, they must work with the union and management to empower every employee to commit to pathogen-free chicken and red meat products. An organizational culture based on trust and clear communication about organizational vision and commitment empowers employees and makes them feel valued.

Max DePree (1989) said that "we must trust one another to be accountable for our own assignments" (p. 116). DePree is aware of what can happen when people begin losing a sense of power over what they produce on the job. Among the signs are the following:

- People begin to have different understandings of words such as *responsibility, service,* and *trust.*
- A dark tension develops among key people.
- Leaders seek to control, rather than liberate.
- Grace, style, and civility are lost.
- People speak of customers as impositions on their time, rather than as opportunities to serve. (pp. 111-112)

Empowerment, then, is based on the richness of relationships among people. Trust and love can never be compromised to gain advantage over others in the family or the workplace. To be empowered, we must be willing to give up our need to control others and learn to trust them and ourselves. Psychologists and theologians say that empowerment begins within each person. Self-love and self-respect are the keys to finding joy in the success of others and recognizing them for their achievements. Self-love and self-respect start with us. If our lives are centered on a power greater than ourselves, we are well on our way toward true empowerment. Without an internal compass that keeps us on ethical paths, empowerment will escape us. Without an internal monitor, we can become possessed by our own importance. Placing ourselves on a pedestal and deceiving ourselves about our own importance lead to arrogance, dishonesty, and a lack of sensitivity to those around us.

Egos can lead the best of us to ruin, and self-empowerment can become a convoluted trail leading to personal and organizational failure. This personal failure can lead to hatred of ourselves and to broken lives. Psychologist Bill Haddock (1998) advises executives of all types of organizations about the power of self-love over self-centeredness. Haddock writes, "When you move from self-centeredness to genuine love for yourself intellectually, physically, emotionally, and spiritually, you learn to love with a higher love, unconditionally. . . . From this kind of inner love you can then love others" (p. 5).

When inner love is balanced with love for others, servant leadership becomes a habit. Theologian Charles Swindoll (1991) suggests two tests of this delicate balance between self-love and love for others:

1. A nondefensive spirit when confronted: This reveals a willingness to be accountable. Genuine humility operates on a rather simple philosophy—nothing to prove and nothing to lose.
2. An authentic desire to help others: I'm referring to a sensitive, spontaneous awareness of needs. A true servant stays in touch with the struggles experienced by others. That is the humility of mind that continually looks for ways to serve and give. (p. 18)

Empowerment for Kids

Wildlife biologist Liz Caldwell lives to empower others in her work in the Oconee Ranger District in Eatonton, Georgia. Liz collaborated with District Ranger Tony Tooke, other colleagues, and community leaders to write grants to help develop wildlife and recreation opportunities for the people of the region. The grants and the servant leadership by the Oconee District employees restored the life and beauty of Miller Creek Lake and a nearby waterfowl area. These developments were realized only because the entire community volunteered to help. County officials, the Macon Bassbusters, local businesses, county extension, senior citizens, the farm bureau, the department of natural resources, schools, and many others came together to make a dream come true.

The dream was to help the kids in the community become involved in environmental education and especially the sport of fishing. To celebrate the pristine Miller Creek Lake improvements, a fishing rodeo was held for all the young people in the area. Fish for the lake were donated by the department of natural resources, local merchants donated hot dogs and

T-shirts with the logo "Get Hooked," and the Zebco Corporation donated tackle boxes to every child and to each school.

The Macon Bassbusters taught the youngsters the finer points of fishing and held a cookout for the entire community. More than 380 young persons benefited from the love of this entire community. The love expressed by Oconee Ranger District employees and many others to restore the natural beauty of Miller Creek Lake and other areas is a powerful example of empowering with love. When I complimented Liz Caldwell on her leadership, she replied,

> It was a labor of love for all of us, and the credit should go to the Forest Service, my mentors, colleagues, local partners, and many others who made this happen. These people have a passion for making life better for others, and that passion played a key role in our success. I am honored to play a small part, and we look forward to several other projects in the coming years. I love what I do because if you can influence one child, you have made success. God is my source of strength, and he guides my every step in educating our future generations to have a love and respect for the outdoors. (personal communication, March 21, 2001)

Liz Caldwell clearly models the following words by William Cunningham (1991), an authority on empowerment: "Relationships are best nourished in a free and open atmosphere in which neither person is interested in pressuring, controlling, or changing the other" (p. 44). To empower is to trust, and to trust is to accept people for who they are and to expect them to give their best effort each day. The best in every person surfaced in Eatonton, Georgia, to help the community become a more loving place.

Empowering others with love is the magic of noble living and human progress. Helen Keller was victorious over her personal challenges because of her optimism and a wonderful, loving teacher, Anne Sullivan, who empowered Helen to write the following words of hope and love: "No pessimist ever discovered the secrets of the stars, or sailed to an uncharted land or opened a new heaven to the human spirit."

Steps Toward Empowering With Love

Step 1: Shine the light on others. The empowering manager succeeds by making everyone else in the organization succeed. For the manager, rewards can be few and far apart. Servant leaders look beyond their rewards and recognition and celebrate in the successes of everyone else in the organization, whether the leaders themselves get any of the credit. Finding joy in the success of others is empowering with love.

Shining the spotlight on others does not dim our leadership role but brightens the entire organization. When in doubt, we should brag about the accomplishments of all employees. Bragging on others' accomplishments is contagious. We like to be around people who compliment us—whether or not we deserve it. If people are complimented frequently, not only are they lifted but also they tend to compliment others. Sometimes a compliment is critical to the success of an organization or team.

Fran Tarkenton, former undersized all-pro quarterback for the Minnesota Vikings, tells about the need for praise. His team was playing a championship game, and the score was close. Coach Bud Grant sent in a play that required the 170-pound Tarkenton to block a 270-pound defensive end to enable his running back to score. Tarkenton threw the block, and a touchdown resulted. He limped to the bench holding his battered ribs while his team was celebrating by throwing helmets into the air and running around giving victory hugs. Not one person said anything to Tarkenton about his key block!

Tarkenton thought to himself that when they viewed the game film, everyone would see his block and say something. The next day while watching the film, he saw his clearing block—again no one said a thing! As the team was leaving the film room, Tarkenton stopped Coach Grant and asked, "Did you see my block?" The coach replied, "Yes." "Why didn't you say something then?" asked Tarkenton. Grant responded, "Fran, you always do your job. I didn't think I had to brag on you." Tarkenton yelled, "If you want me to do it again, you will!" (Martin, 1994, pp. 118-119; used by permission). When in doubt, brag—don't nag. We empower others through trust and telling them that we believe in them and the job they do.

Step 2: Provide the necessary resources to all employees. The empowering manager knows that the people in the organization need resources to do their jobs. Some of these resources require materials and supplies that stretch beyond the organization's budget. To empower others to be successful, you must be the primary advocate for getting the necessary resources from upper management, placing your own reputation on the line by calling in past favors to see that eager employees get the materials they need. Empowering others with love means taking calculated risks to provide the resources to produce quality and create customer satisfaction.

Brigadier General Don Flickinger, manager for the Mercury Space Program, found and trained seven astronauts—Alan Shepard, Virgil "Gus" Grissom, John Glenn, Scott Carpenter, Wally Schirra, Gordon Cooper, and Donald "Deke" Slayton. They were given the best training possible and supplied with the most up-to-date equipment for the training and the actual flights.

As program chief, Flickinger empowered himself to take the necessary risks and inspire many others to provide his program and the seven astronauts with the needed resources to venture into space. This act of empowering with love rallied a nation to raise the funds to train the astronauts and provide the technologies. On May 15, 1963, the United States caught the Soviet Union in the race for space. Americans everywhere felt empowered by these monumental space ventures, and U.S. astronauts landed on the moon six years later (Buckingham & Coffman, 1999, p. 74).

Step 3: Open the doors of opportunity for all employees. Never assume that your employees are satisfied with their job roles for the rest of their working lives. It is easier for managers to categorize individuals in specific roles on the basis of some preconceived notion of who they are and their level of education. This preconception hit home when an elementary school principal told me that his best first-grade teacher was a fantastic teacher because she looked like a first-grade teacher and teaching is all she wanted to do. I asked the principal if he had ever asked the teacher about her career goals, and his response was, "Well, no, I have not—I don't want to lose her."

Research conducted in the Edinburg (Texas) Independent School District revealed alarming results about principals ignoring career aspirations of their teachers. More than 300 teachers responded to the Staff Sensitivity Scale item "How often does your principal discuss your career goals?" More than 80% responded *rarely or never.* Another item asked, "How often does your principal share power?" Again, the majority of the teachers responded, *rarely or never* (Hoyle & Oates, 1998).

What does this say about empowering with love? Leaders need to ask employees about their career goals, introduce them to important people, provide professional development opportunities for growth, and never assume that an employee is happy with his or her job status. One of my joys as a professor is to take graduate students to state and national conferences and introduce them to the big names in research and professional practice. These opportunities to rub shoulders with the power brokers can pay off in big dividends for my students in jobs, publications, and consulting opportunities.

Baseball and Empowering With Love

A story told by Rabbi Paysach Krohn exemplifies empowerment. The father of a disabled boy was invited to speak at a fundraiser for a private school in Brooklyn, New York. The father began talking about perfection and the difficulty that some kids have in reaching anything near perfection. He talked about his boy, Shaya, who was not perfect nor capable of learning as fast or performing physical activities as well as more perfect kids. He told about the previous weekend when he and his son went to see a baseball game at his school. A good crowd had gathered to watch the two teams compete for the all-school championship. During the second inning, Shaya looked up at his dad and asked, "Do you think they would let me play?" His dad said, "Go ask one of the team captains if it is possible." Shaya slowly walked up to the larger boy and inquired about playing in the game. The team captain shook his head and said, "Maybe next game."

Shaya's father told the banquet audience that the look on his little boy's face nearly broke his heart. The next inning, the father walked up to another large boy and asked him, "Do you think Shaya could get into the game for a little while?" The boy hesitated and looked over at Shaya and responded, "Well, we are six runs down and it is the seventh inning so tell Shaya to get a glove and play short right field next inning." Shaya borrowed a glove and slowly made his way to the outfield.

The next inning, his team scored three runs to put his team only three runs behind. Three of his teammates loaded the bases with two outs in the bottom of the ninth inning. It was Shaya's time to bat. Because he had never used a bat, he was sure that the team would replace him for a pinch hitter. The larger teammate who let him play looked at Shaya and told him, "Grab a bat." As Shaya slowly walked up to the plate, the pitcher, seeing Shaya's physical limitations, moved up a few feet in front of the mound and pitched underhand to him. Shaya swung with all his might only to miss the ball by six inches. Suddenly, a teammate ran out of the dugout, placed his arms around Shaya, and helped him hold the bat. On the next pitch, they hit a weak grounder back to the pitcher. Shaya's teammates and the crowd were screaming, "Run! Run to first base!" The pitcher watched Shaya's attempt to run, and rather than throwing to first base to end the game, he threw the ball far over the first baseman's reach, and the ball bounced down the foul line to the right fielder. By this time, Shaya's teammates and the crowd were yelling, "Run to second! Run to second!" The other three runners were circling the bases for home when the right fielder picked up the ball and, sensing what the pitcher had done, threw the ball far over third base down the left field line. When

Shaya reached second base, the crowd yelled, "Run to third! Run to third!" Not knowing what to do, Shaya stopped at second. The shortstop grabbed him by the shoulders, turned him toward third base, and yelled, "Run to third! Run to third!" When Shaya reached third base, all eight of his teammates and nine players from the other team on the field were running behind Shaya yelling, "Run for home! Run for home!" With tears in his eyes, the father tells the audience that Shaya ran as fast as he could and slid into home plate for the winning run. In a spirit of great joy, 17 boys picked Shaya up on their shoulders and paraded him around the field as their hero. The father then told the audience, "I do not know why all kids are not made perfect, but last Saturday, I saw perfection in 17 boys who made my Shaya feel perfect for that wonderful moment" (Krohn, 1999).[1]

Empowering with love comes from the depths of our hearts and souls. When you empower others, you empower yourself tenfold.

Mahatma Gandhi empowered millions, although he was not a gifted artist, scholar, or scientist; never earned a degree from a prestigious university; and never held a political office. When he died in 1948, however, the world mourned him (Edelman, 1992).

> *Our minds have the potential of either using or throwing away all the power we possess. As empowered people we are able to enjoy and profit by the world because we are able to respond to it in a natural way. This is the legacy of empowerment.*
>
> —William C. Cunningham, 1991, p. 135

Note

1. Reproduced from *Maggid Speaks: Favorite Stories and Parables of Rabbi Shalom Schwadron,* by Rabbi Paysach Krohn, with permission from the copyright holders, ArtScroll/Mesorah Publications, Ltd.

6

Mentoring With Love

A mentor gives from the heart, teaches from experience, demands our best effort, accepts our failures, forgives our ungratefulness, and smiles when we succeed.

—John R. Hoyle

Behind every successful person is a mentor or mentors. These giants in our lives are there to inspire, teach, advise, introduce us to important people, recommend us for jobs, and listen when we talk. Mentors keep us from drifting off course by reminding us of who we are, what we do best, and how we can succeed. Kevin Hogan (2000), author of *Talk Your Way to the Top*, found that 70% of all executives promoted in 1998 were mentored on their path to the top. History records the value of mentors in ancient Greece. In Homer's *Odyssey*, Mentor was the teacher entrusted by Odysseus to tutor his son, Telemachus (Lewis, 2001).

Socrates mentored Plato, Plato mentored Aristotle, and Aristotle mentored Alexander the Great. Gamaliel mentored the apostle Paul, Emerson shared his literary gifts with Thoreau, and Martin Luther King Jr. mentored Andrew Young. Civil rights leader Daisy Bates, mentioned earlier in Chapter 1, mentored with love nine black students who broke the color barrier at Little Rock Central High School in 1957. Helen Keller tells about her mentor, Anne Sullivan, who, near death, was told that she must get well because without her, Helen would be nothing. "That would mean," Anne Sullivan replied, "that I had failed."

Definition of Mentoring

Del Wasden (1988) at Brigham Young University defines mentoring this way:

> The mentor is a master at providing opportunities for growth of others by identifying situations and events which contribute knowledge and experience to the life of the mentee. Opportunities are not happenstance; they must be thoughtfully designed and organized into logical sequence. Sometimes hazards are attached to opportunity. The mentor takes great pains to help the mentee recognize and negotiate dangerous situations. In doing this, the mentor has an opportunity for growth though service, which is the highest form of leadership. (p. 3)

Successful mentoring occurs when "top-level executives teach selected junior persons the rules of the game; provide opportunities for them to demonstrate their skill; challenge them; give them critical feedback; and if ready, sponsor them into higher level positions" (Mertz, Welch, & Henderson, 1990, p. 7). Sylvia Hornbeck, a human resource specialist for the Energy Worldnet, a natural gas company, relates how Pat Riley, manager of Gibson County (Tennessee) Utility District, mentors others and leads by example.

Riley was deeply concerned that gas prices in some parts of the country had increased by more than 100%, forcing some businesses to close or consolidate. Many fixed- or low-income people could no longer afford to pay their gas bills. Riley spoke out about natural gas prices with a deep concern for people struggling to pay their gas bills. He said,

> It just breaks your heart when you hear a customer on the phone asking whether they should pay their gas bill or buy prescription medicines and, in some cases, food. These folks don't know anything about wellhead prices, underground storage, or import quotas and tariffs. It's awful hard for them to get terribly distraught over environmentally sensitive tundra in Alaska when their thermostat is set below 60 degrees in order to save enough on their gas bills to add a few more essential items to their shopping carts. We just try to help them as best we can. We even implemented two new policies in order to help our customers. These new policies include delaying payment and paying half of the amount due and the remaining half the next billing cycle. (Public Gas Association, 2001, p. 2)

Sylvia told me, "Pat Riley is a role model to all of us in the industry because of his love for people and his abilities to balance that love while keeping an eye on the bottom line."

The Pain and Pleasure of Mentoring

In guiding Barbara, a graduate student, through a difficult time, university professor Richard applied mentoring with love, service, and critical feedback. Barbara was an applicant for an associate manager's position with a software company that produced educational materials for corporate and educational training. Barbara's mentor, Richard, knew the company CEO, Ralph, who during a phone call assured Richard that Barbara was their number one candidate before her job interview.

The interview team consisted of the vice president for personnel, two associate managers, and five work team members. Barbara was excited about the interview and felt some comfort in the thought that it was her job to lose. Richard told Barbara to "be yourself and show them what a talented and wonderful person you are. Call me when you return from the interview and let me know how it went."

Two days later, Barbara came to Richard's office and declared,

> I think I blew them away. I told them about my management style and how I demanded the best from myself and others on the team. The group interview was rather sedate, but they seemed to like what I had to say. My exit interview with the CEO led me to believe that the job was mine and that I should hear from the vice president for personnel very soon.

Richard was happy for Barbara and felt that his personal friendship with the CEO was a key to the good news.

The following Monday, Barbara knocked on Richard's office door, and Richard responded, "Come on in here!" Richard looked up at Barbara to hear the good news. Barbara's face was not victorious—she looked like a student who had flunked out of school. Richard asked, "Well, what is the latest about the job offer?" With tears in her eyes and halting speech, Barbara said, "They gave the job to someone else. They hired an insider who had only a bachelor's degree, and the vice president told me, 'It was a difficult decision between you and the other candidate, but we feel his experiences in software development and sales were more extensive.' "

Richard felt bad for Barbara and started to hug and console her but instead held her hand and said, "I'm so sorry about this news, but they are the ones who should be sorry for misleading you and for hiring someone less qualified." Richard knew his words were of little comfort when he said, "Barbara, this wasn't the job you were meant to have. Another opportunity will come up that will be much better for you and your professional career."

After Barbara left the office, Richard called his friend Ralph about the situation. Richard asked Ralph if he could share information about Barbara's interview that he could use to help her in future interviews. Ralph said,

> Barbara came across with other top management and me as a go-getter with a bright and creative mind. However, the interview team of peers and subordinates felt that Barbara was too assertive and perhaps insensitive in her remarks about her expectations about each person striving for continuous improvement and using data rather than personal opinion for all decision making.
>
> Barbara was dressed like a poor graduate student and did not exude a strong feeling of self-confidence. As you know, Richard, in these days of shared decision making, the CEO has the final say on a hire, but when a key work team fails to agree on their leader, I have to lean toward their preferences.

Richard was silent for a few seconds, trying to keep his anger under control, and finally said, "Well, Barbara is really hurt over this, and I wish I had known before her interview that she was one of two candidates and the one selected had been with your office for two years. Thanks for the information and for considering Barbara."

Richard shared with Barbara the information about the interview and the other hurtful comments. After a short pause, Barbara thanked Richard for his help and the information. She then asked, "What can I do to make a better impression next time?" Richard gave her words of advice about language to use in interviews that would inspire confidence, rather than uncertainty. Next, he asked Barbara if she would like to participate in a mock interview to help practice her skills. She agreed, and Richard replied, "Let's set up a mock interview with a couple of faculty members and two Exxon recruiters who will be on campus next Tuesday. One of the Exxon people is also an expert on dressing for success."

The mock interview was helpful in assisting Barbara in improving her interpersonal and communication skills, and she accepted an offer by Richard for a small loan to help her purchase a business suit for her next interview. Two weeks later, Barbara interviewed with a larger software company and was hired as a product manager for a bigger salary and greater promise of promotion than the initial position. In three years,

Barbara was selected as a vice president for marketing, and she hired Richard as a consultant to teach mentoring skills to company managers.

Mentoring and Commitment

Mentoring means commitment to those who are mentored. Once we as mentors agree to take on the responsibilities and joys of mentoring, we are personally obligated to assist the protégé in times of difficulty and success. My mentor, Dr. Paul Hensarling, helped shape my career and attitudes toward people and life. During my doctoral studies, he appointed me to teach an undergraduate class to help me prepare for a career in higher education. Dr. Hensarling observed my teaching and made many helpful suggestions to improve my classroom effectiveness in teaching strategies, projects, and assessment. At one point during those three long and arduous years, I thought about quitting and finding a real job because my wife had no new clothes, our car was wearing out, and my self-esteem was tumbling. I walked into his office and announced that I was thinking about quitting the program and going to work to make some money for my family. He looked at me a moment and responded with words that changed my life forever. He said, "John, you have no idea how talented you are. Remember, just be better than you think you can be." That's all he said. I stood up, shook his hand, and left his office with a resolve to live up to his words.

The awesome power of mentoring with love has driven legions of individuals to greatness in industry, government, education, coaching, and the ministry. I regret that my mentor was not present in August 1999 when my colleagues at the National Conference of Professors of Educational Administration selected me for the first Living Legend Award. This award should also include the name Paul R. Hensarling.

James Kouzes and Barry Posner (1995) remind us about the importance of mentors in our lives and how they teach us the skills, craft knowledge, and how to play the game when necessary. Mentors can save their protégés some grief by sharing their experiences learned in the school of hard knocks. A wise and trusted mentor is more important than immediate supervisors, managers, and peers.

Executive Mentoring

Who will take your place when you retire or leave for another executive position? Have you been a mentor for one or more protégés who have the attributes to be successful, or have you detached yourself from those eager to fill your position?

Margaret, a fast-food chain executive, had no family member to follow in her footsteps. She mentored two eager young regional managers to prepare them for her position when she retired. She invited them to sit in on all executive meetings where confidential financial and franchise issues were discussed, arranged one-on-one mentoring with each protégé, invited them to attend national and international stockholder meetings, spent time with them in their offices, and invited them to dinners and social gatherings.

Although charges of favoritism were made by the other ignored regional managers, she chose to mentor the two with the greatest potential to fill her CEO position. One of her protégés was selected by the corporate board for the CEO position, and the fast-food company continued its number one position under new leadership.

In contrast, Ralph, a school superintendent in a large suburban school district, refused to mentor anyone to fill his position when he retired or left the district for another superintendency. He felt that if he mentored two of his most popular and talented subordinates, they would gain access to his private information and spread rumors about his district plans and personnel decisions about principals and central office administrators. Ralph hired a consultant to devise an organizational chart that clearly detailed the chain of command with him at the top of the chain. With the new Machiavellian plan, Ralph kept information about the district close to his chest and told the assistant superintendents to communicate with the school principals. Although Ralph rarely got out of his office to visit a school, he was visible in the community as a member of the chamber of commerce, Rotary Club, and the largest church in town. He thought of himself as a corporate CEO and as a manipulator of power over all school matters.

When test scores in the district began dropping and key administrators began leaving the district, Ralph turned to his staff for help. Community unrest increased, and Ralph took all the heat for the district failures. Because he had chosen not to mentor talented protégés and share information about the district and his plans, no one had good information to share with the stakeholders. Ralph had failed to build his executive team and a strong network of staff to help solve the district performance and low morale problems that drove people from the district. Unlike Margaret, Ralph had failed to mentor executives who could step up and assist him in times of difficulty.

According to Mertz et al. (1990), executive mentoring "provides a vehicle through which an organization can develop one of its most important resources—human potential. When that potential is fully utilized, it contributes significantly to organizational longevity and growth" (p. 10). Mertz et al. continue by listing five benefits of mentoring for the organization and the executive:

1. Mentoring builds a positive organizational climate. A positive organizational climate is called *esprit de corps* rather than *love,* but love is the key to caring about the potential and professional aspirations of each employee.
2. Mentoring provides a mechanism for rewarding managers. Managers create a positive tone by mentoring and promoting people with the talent and desire to succeed. By rewarding these individuals, management will benefit by higher-performing organizations.
3. Mentoring builds a pool of ready talent. Individuals within the organization including women, minorities, and white males who may not fit the traditional image of top managers must be given the opportunities to advance. Rather than searching for talent outside the organization, encouraging the potential within ensures continuity and morale.
4. Mentoring demonstrates what is valued. The behaviors that managers model for others set the tone in the organization. Good mentoring sends positive signals that high-quality performance will be rewarded.
5. Mentoring opens channels of communication. When trust is established between mentor and protégé, the real issues and problems of the organization can be discussed. Mentoring creates an upward flow of information that is usually filtered in organizations. (pp. 10-13)

Mentoring Women

Women are often overlooked in executive searches in all fields, and there is little doubt about the salary differentiation between women and men. Perhaps the major factor in this salary gap is the popular view that mentoring is gender specific. The prevailing reasons that men are selected over women for executive positions are the "good old boy" network and limited mentoring opportunities for women protégés. According to management scholars George Dreher and Ronald Ash (1990), mentoring is not necessarily gender specific. They write, "Because few women hold advanced managerial positions, male managers are more likely to serve as mentors" (p. 539). Despite a salary difference of $7,990 between male and female business school graduates, Dreher and Ash found,

> Predictions regarding gender-specific exposure to mentoring experiences and the moderating effects of gender on relationships between mentoring and career outcomes were not supported by these data. The results run counter to the notion that women are not well integrated into the mentoring systems. Therefore, although mentoring relationships may contribute to career success, they do not account for the observed income difference between men and women. (p. 544)

As in any research findings about the role of men and women in the workforce, caution is the watchword.

Despite an increasing number of talented women in managerial positions, research findings about mentoring for women who reach executive positions are mixed. Although the salary gap between male and female executives is narrowing in upper-level managerial positions, research targeting mentoring and salary differences among women in midlevel management is unclear.

Psychologists Bell Ragins and Eric Sundstrom (1989) observed that although both men and women are moving toward occupations traditionally held by men, "Women may still be segregated into female-type specializations that offer few resources for power than do male-type specialties" (p. 56). Companies recognize the need for mentoring all types of managers, but most well-designed mentoring activities are directed only toward top executives, senior managers, and high potentials (Caudron, 2000). Therefore, few conclusions can be made about the impact of mentoring programs on lower-level managerial positions because size and type of organization and the differences between managerial positions that demand higher levels of expertise cloud the findings.

It is obvious to me that as long as men hold the majority of top managerial positions in business, education, government, and medicine, women aiming at the top must look to both men and women as mentors in their path to top management. Geraldine Spruell (1985) found that Clare Longden, first vice president and certified financial planner at Butcher and Singer, believes that men mentoring women are not always sure of what to look for in a women trying to reach a higher management post. She doesn't believe that it is conscious discrimination but that women "have not been in the work force long enough to achieve many senior positions. . . . Men's way of thinking just hasn't caught up with all the changes in the work place" (p. 31). Role models for women aspiring to top leadership positions can be either gender, but the force of love in the mentoring process is the motivating force.

Larry Lewis (2001), an area superintendent in the Austin (Texas) Independent School District, conducted a study to investigate the effect of gender on an induction-year mentoring program experience as perceived by selected female principals and their mentors. Lewis found that as first-year principals, women have less authority and influence than do men and may not get as much accomplished in their first year. The protégés were aware of how gender was perceived by men, maybe their mentors, and others in general. The protégés spoke of being considered a "bitch" for pushing too much for their schools and of not being considered real principals because of their gender.

The male mentors perceived the protégés as emotional, weak, and unable to get some things done because of their gender. The most interesting finding, according to Lewis (2001), was on communications: "The interviews clearly show that every protégé and mentor had a concern about gender and/or race, but these concerns were not discussed at all in the mentoring relationships" (p. 148). Lewis concludes that people tend to be "blind to the effect of their culture or socialization experiences on their interpretation of gender in mentoring relationships, and gender impacts same-sex mentoring relationships in that some protégés with female mentors were concerned about competition and trust" (p. 152).

These findings add evidence that gender does make a difference in mentoring. Although mentors may claim that they treat all their protégés the same, research reveals that being kind, being a good listener, and having connections are not enough to successfully mentor men and women. Mentoring with love is finding the barriers that women and some men encounter in the job market and guiding them around the barriers.

Donald Clifton and Paula Nelson (1992), authors of *Soar With Your Strengths*, believe that regardless of gender in the mentoring process, relationships must be positive. They write, "Relationship is the process of investing in another person by doing things for that person's own good without consideration of self-reward. Ultimately, it is the sum of our responses to another human being" (p. 124).

Mentoring Minorities

Although the term *minority* is slowly disappearing from our lexicon, minority status is a reality for many seeking equity and fairness in employment opportunities in most organizations. When minority managers are underrepresented in organizations, mentoring by majority managers takes on a new and vital role. Although most well-meaning and caring mentors believe that race and background are factors to be considered, they may believe that the ethnicity of their protégé is not that important. Mentors assume that their minority protégés all have the same desire to climb the ladder to top positions and are willing to pay the work price to get there. Well-intentioned mentors overlook the cultural perspectives of protégés about success and rank in organizations. Mentors can fall into the trap of applying different performance evaluation standards for minority groups, rather than judging the individual.

Mentors may feel uncomfortable mentoring someone from a different social or cultural background and fail to openly communicate the protégé's worth and potential. Another mistake by mentors is making offensive remarks or misguided humor directed at the protégé without understanding the damage created in the mentoring relationship. To mentor a minority protégé and not invite him or her to social and professional gatherings is a grievous mistake. Also, good mentors mix and mingle with members of minority groups, rather than isolate themselves with individuals of the same race and color (Mertz et al., 1990).

Mentors from the majority race fall into race blindness when they think about their replacements. These replacements are usually those men or perhaps women who are in their immediate management circles. "Out of sight, out of mind" can lead to an all-majority selection process for a position despite the call for minority candidates in the job announcement.

Love is the guiding force in mentoring minority protégés. Love will open the lines of communication between the mentor and protégé to help them embrace cultural and social differences to build a stronger learning organization. A European American mentor can never really understand what it is to be African American, Native American, Mexican American, or Asian American; the mentor, however, has an ethical and professional obligation to listen, mix, read, and attend multicultural gatherings to gain the feelings of difference and sameness. Thus, as the workforce becomes more diverse, the process of mentoring women and minorities for executive positions becomes more vital to organizational development.

According to University of Texas counseling psychologists Lucia Gilbert and Karen Rossman (1992), "Little has been written examining the mentoring process for these diverse groups. In particular, the experiences of women of color as mentors and protégés remain relatively unaddressed" (p. 237). My colleagues from different ethnic heritages tell me that "having a good heart" is the first step in mentoring a minority or a majority protégé. A good heart can guide the head to view difference as a gift to the organization and to the management team.

Mentoring and Victory

Grant Teaff (personal communication, April 14, 1995), former football coach at Baylor University, tells a story about the magic of mentoring with love. In the spring of 1972, Coach Teaff asked a skinny sophomore quarterback to come to his office with three written personal and team goals. The bashful athlete walked into the office and handed Teaff the three goals and began trying to orally repeat the goals. A speech impediment or stutter, however, made for a prolonged report. Grant Teaff listened as the youngster told him that his goal was to quarterback the Baylor Bears to the first Southwest Conference championship in more than 50 years and lead the team to the Cotton Bowl.

After a brief pause while looking into the intense eyes of the young man, Teaff said, "Son, what can I do to help you accomplish your dream?" The coach could have said, "I'm sorry, son, but you and I know that you can't reach your goal as a quarterback with your speech problem." During the quarterback's first season, teammates called the signals in the huddle; in his junior year, he claims that he frequently sang the signals to avoid stuttering.

His senior year, Neal Jeffrey clearly called the signals himself and led the Baylor Bears to the first Southwest Conference championship in more than 50 years and to the Cotton Bowl. This 1974 team and its determined quarterback became known as the "Miracle on the Brazos." Neal Jeffrey is now a successful and articulate minister in Dallas, Texas (Hoyle, 1995, pp. 43-44). Mentoring another person to success is the highest form of love, and that love led Neal Jeffrey to a life of servant leadership and to mentoring thousands of young people.

The "Mentor's Pledge" shown in Box 6.1, an adaptation of another pledge on management, will help you remember the key points of mentoring protégés in any situation. On the basis of this pledge, what type of mentor are you? In Box 6.2, discover your mentoring IQ/EI (Emotional Intelligence; Goleman, 1997) by responding to the 10 items and using the scoring range of 50 to 10 points.

> *Every person passing through this life will unknowingly leave something and take something away. Most of the "something" cannot be seen or heard or numbered. But nothing counts without it.*
>
> —Robert Fulghum, 1989, p. 119

BOX 6.1
Mentor's Pledge

To set the right example for your protégés by your actions

To be consistent in your temperament so that your protégés will know how to read you and what they can expect from you

To be fair, impartial, and consistent in matters relating to work rules, discipline, and rewards

To show a sincere, personal interest in your protégés without becoming overly familiar

To seek your protégés' counsel on matters affecting their jobs and to be guided as much as possible by their judgment

To allow your protégés as much individuality as possible in the way their jobs are performed, as long as the quality of the end result is not compromised

To make your protégés always know in advance what you expect from them in the way of conduct and performance on the job

To be appreciative of your protégés' efforts and generous in praise of their accomplishments

To use every opportunity to teach your protégés how to do their jobs better and how to help themselves advance in skill level and responsibility

To show your protégés that you can "do" as well as "manage" by pitching in to work beside them when your help is needed

SOURCE: Author unknown.

BOX 6.2
Your Mentoring IQ/EI Scale

Give yourself four points if you check *always,* three points for *usually,* two points for *sometimes,* and one point for *rarely.*

When mentoring protégés, do you listen more than you talk?
_____ always _____ usually _____ sometimes _____ rarely

Are you fair, impartial, and consistent while mentoring your protégés in matters relating to work rules, discipline, and rewards?
_____ always _____ usually _____ sometimes _____ rarely

Do you actively seek out protégés to mentor?
_____ always _____ usually _____ sometimes _____ rarely

Do you mentor only protégés who look like you (gender and race)?
_____ always _____ usually _____ sometimes _____ rarely

Are you comfortable mentoring persons with different accents or cultures?
_____ always _____ usually _____ sometimes _____ rarely

Do you seek out protégés who are less popular among your peers?
_____ always _____ usually _____ sometimes _____ rarely

Do you make sure that your protégés know in advance what you expect from them in their conduct and performance on the job?
_____ always _____ usually _____ sometimes _____ rarely

When you feel a personal conflict between you and your protégés, do you maintain a caring, sensitive attitude?
_____ always _____ usually _____ sometimes _____ rarely

Do you feel that you have the skills to be a good mentor?
_____ always _____ usually _____ sometimes _____ rarely

Do you introduce your protégés to important people and provide other avenues for networking?
_____ always _____ usually _____ sometimes _____ rarely

Your IQ/EQ score:

50-40 Bright Mentor, 39-30 Average Mentor, 29-10 Repeat Mentor Training

The Sixth Key
Evaluating With Love

*Taking an interest in the soul is a way of loving it. The ultimate
cure, as many ancients and modern psychologies of depth have
asserted, comes from love and not logic.*

—Thomas Moore, 1992, p. 14

"What gets measured gets done." This familiar quote reflects public interest in holding organizations and individuals accountable. David Osborne and Ted Gaebler (1992) write, "Words like 'accountability,' 'performance,' and 'results' have begun to ring through the hall of government" (p. 14). They believe that results-oriented government has changed from politics and fiscal inputs to program outcomes and effectiveness.

Evaluating the performance of organizations and individuals is an inexact science that can be fear inducing. When accrediting and auditing agencies come calling to evaluate a school, university, hospital, or business, anxieties run high. What if we fail the audit or lose our accreditation or our jobs? Will the inspectors find our product below industry standards? Will the IRS find discrepancies? The fears usually heighten when the boss conducts his or her annual evaluation of our performance in sales, teaching, nursing, surgery, meat inspecting, or banking. Did we meet our targeted goals? Did we maintain good interpersonal relations with our customers, students, or patients?

According to human resource consultant Robert Maddux (2000), this fear of evaluation is justified.

> Modern managers have been caught in a whirlpool of change that has often diminished their financial resources, reduced their staff, cut their training budget, and increased their personal work load. They have witnessed, and often presided over, the elimination of layers of management and support staff that included many friends and trusted associates. (p. 13)

Although economic realities hover over most organizations, fear and evaluation need not be synonymous if the evaluator relies on human factors, research findings, best practices, and unconditional love for those being evaluated. If finding fault in the employee's performance, rather than locating the areas in need of improvement, is the focus of the evaluation, then the evaluation is a nonloving force.

The evaluator who lets love guide personnel evaluations will look for positive behaviors and accomplishments while attempting to identify areas of low performance or behaviors that detract from accomplishing personal and organizational goals. Evaluations guided by love are difficult for overachievers who really believe in the 20/80 "rule," that is, 20% of the people do 80% of the work (Carlson, 1998, p. 57).

Psychologist David McClelland (1978) found that some individuals are driven to achieve and have little tolerance for those who are not so driven. This intolerance can play out in negative comments about slothful coworkers who fail to produce their fair share and can lead to performance evaluation systems with unrealistic expectations of all employees. The overachiever evaluator without love will use unrealistic work standards to judge each employee and will eventually create irreparable damage to morale.

Richard Carlson (1998) puts this problem of job performance variation in perspective with these questions: "Do I base my productivity choices on what others think I should be doing? Am I attempting to frustrate and irritate others by the pace of my work?" Carlson believes that "your choices are the result of your own rhythm, preferred pace of work, and desired results" (p. 59).

Victor Vroom (1964) provides the underlying theory about individual choice in work productivity in his expectancy theory. He believes that positive or negative attitudes about the job task (valence), the incentives forthcoming from completing the task (instrumentality), and the personal satisfaction of knowing that the work effort will help the worker become a higher performer (expectancy) are the key forces in worker productivity. Individuals differ in their perceptions of the jobs they do on the basis of the rewards that they expect for their performance. Evaluators should remember that they would also be evaluated by other overachievers in top management who also have choices.

Evaluation Is to Value

The definition of *evaluation* is to determine the value of something and determine its worthiness. People must be valued over the organization because their personal needs, dispositions, and dreams should drive performance evaluations of employees and the organization.

Jim McCann, the "Flower Guy" and CEO of 1-800-Flowers, is a model leader who evaluates his employees' values. He took his company from the edge of bankruptcy to a $300 million business that ranks as the world's largest florist. McCann says,

> While it is true that there are a lot of ruthless types who make a success of themselves, I have found that it is just as true that building relationships with people was the only way that I was able to forge ahead. . . . Given a choice, folks will always choose to do business with the people and companies that value them. (McCann & Kaminsky, 1998, pp. 239-240)

When people are valued and trusted, they become part of the driving vision of excellence and welcome evaluations that help them become more productive each year.

Buckingham and Coffman (1999) found four characteristics common to the performance management routines of great managers. First, they keep the process simple; second, they plan frequent interactions between themselves and the employee; third, they focus on the future; and fourth, they ask the employee to keep a record of his or her own performance and professional development (pp. 222-223). Thus, great managers value their employees and focus on how to help them perform at higher levels by offering opportunities for them to "sharpen their saws" and feel pride in being part of a winning team.

The Art of Evaluating With Love

Evaluation specialists have struggled for more than 150 years to design a state-of-the-art personnel evaluation system. Several models have been created, but none removes the subjective judgments by those doing the judging. The job target, 360-degree, management by objectives, and mutual benefit models have become the most common, and a blend of these models are found in most personnel evaluation systems. The 360-degree assessment model has gained wide acceptance in all types of organizations. Polaris International North designed a management development program that begins with a 360-degree assessment of each manager's skills.

According to editor Shari Caudron (2000), the 360-degree model has three powerful elements:

1. Each manager receives one-on-one coaching and development training.
2. Participants develop an external support network consisting of their peers in other member firms.
3. Trainees are assigned mentors in their own firms to talk with about the course material and ongoing feedback on their own abilities. (p. 30)

Richard Daft (1983) explains that performance evaluation systems in the business world are typically centered on goals determined primarily by management and used to establish performance levels of employees for a given period. Managers monitor employee performance to guide personnel decisions on promotion, dismissal, and professional development needs of individuals and groups.

Evaluation systems of the organizations are not the problem— human judgment is. Unloving evaluators can make evaluation data fit their personal whims, likes, and dislikes and paint a picture of the person being evaluated as a blooming flower or a dying weed. Chuck, a skilled maintenance employee in a large state university, was asked if love had any place in his annual performance evaluation. Without hesitation, Chuck smiled and said, "Are you kidding? There is no love in my evaluation; it's dog-eat-dog."

Evaluation systems used as control devices by top management can lead to what management gurus call *clan control* (Daft, 1983). Noel Tichy and Mary Anne Devanna (1990) report that the most reliable performance assessment comes from a person's subordinates and peers. Despite this knowledge, the majority of corporations, universities, banking institutions, schools, and government agencies are unwilling to implement a system in which peers and subordinates evaluate people in the organization.

School superintendents use clan control by hiring and promoting family members and friends of board members and staff; labor unions are guilty of hiring and promoting family members of longtime members; corporations are guilty of hiring and promoting those who fit the corporate image and have been socialized into the culture of the organization. Clan control is blatant in the political appointments of rich campaign contributors. These methods of favoritism in hiring, promoting, and appointing are woven into the fabric of organizational life.

One of the best ways to destroy morale is to compare the performance of individuals within the organization. Author Gifford Pinchot (1985) writes about unfair performance comparisons: "Once the invidious comparison is made, the invidious game begins. The solution is to compare people with their counterparts outside the company, not with others inside it. This places the focus on the real competition of the corporation" (p. 236). The best evaluation systems will never eliminate all these human frailties, but goal-based, objective performance systems that rely on good data from a variety of sources help offset human subjectivity in personnel performance assessment.

Assessment Centers

In tracing the historical development of assessment centers, George Thornton and William Byham (1983) found that the centers have made strides in evaluating personnel performance in a more valid, reliable, and systematic way. They found that personnel are more satisfied with and stay with the organization longer if assessment centers are in place. Also, assessment centers produce more accurate predictions of managerial success than traditional paper-and-pencil tests and personality profile measures.

According to Thornton and Byham (1983), an assessment center is "a comprehensive, standardized procedure in which multiple assessment techniques such as situational exercises and job simulations (i.e., business games, discussion groups, reports, and presentations) are used to evaluate individual employees for various purposes" (p. 1). Robert Guion (1998), an expert on personnel assessment, is not as supportive of assessment centers as are Thornton and Byham. Although assessment centers are widely used in a variety of organizations, research findings about their success are mixed. Guion reports that corrected validity coefficients for predicting personnel performance using assessment centers were .36 to .53. He asks, "Why would one go to the trouble and expense of developing an assessment center that, on the average, might yield a lower validity rating than achieved by less expensive, more traditional methods?" (p. 666). Guion and others are not advocating the dismantling of assessment centers but recommend the need for further research to improve effectiveness.

A typical assessment center has highly trained assessors who observe and evaluate candidates in various exercises and simulations. In the early

1980s, the National Association of Secondary School Principals (NASSP) created an assessment center that evaluated participants on 12 skill dimensions: problem analysis, judgment, organizational ability, decisiveness, leadership, sensitivity, stress tolerance, written communication, oral communication, personal motivation, range of interests, and educational values. Research on the NASSP assessment effort (Schmitt & Cohen, 1990) shows that assessment centers help identify promising candidates for the position of principal because the overall ratings received by those assessed are valid, reliable, and related to the real day-to-day job of a principal.

The centers are expensive and labor-intensive to operate, however. The cost per individual ranges from $500 to $1,500, and the skills (standards) established for benchmark performance have not been consistently tested. Studies reveal mixed results as to the effectiveness of assessment centers compared with more conventional methods. Until the validity coefficients are consistently stronger, as stated earlier by Guion, other assessment methods are needed that are more valid and less expensive to predict and measure successful personnel performance on the job. Personnel specialists believe that the best indicator of success for any employee is his or her career achievements through time. The past, however, may not be the best indicator if the individual has been in a different role within the organization or is coming from the outside. Unfortunately, research findings provide limited guidance in predicting how successful a person will be in the actual workplace, especially in daily interpersonal relations and other work habits vital to successful job performance.

No Perfect Evaluation System

No system gives a total performance and personality profile, and the chances of a perfect system are remote. For instance, an academic department in a large state university recently filled a faculty position with a "bright young star" who had an impressive record of publications, presentations, and research grants. "Star" was given the highest recommendations from colleagues and scholars; administrators from other universities extolled Star's scholarly productivity and high academic standards. Star had received tenure the previous year and negotiated coming in with tenure and an attractive salary package. The only hint of a performance problem was offered by a colleague about Star's "sometimes unrealistic standards for students."

Within the first year, the complaints from students about Star's unrealistic standards and negative attitude toward students became a headache for the department head and some faculty advisers. Star's reputation spread among the students, and class enrollments dwindled. Initially, Star could not understand why students complained about high standards and expectations. Star told the students and colleagues, "I have high standards, and I am not going to compromise them." Senior faculty and the department chair listened to Star's concern and offered suggestions about ways to maintain high standards by more deliberate alignment of the reading and research assignments with exams and research papers.

Star considered the suggestions and became more student oriented, a better teacher, and a better member of the department. Within a year, class enrollments grew. This story can be told about other organizations in which job expectations are unclear, assessment data are limited, competition is strong, and professional development opportunities are lacking.

Performance evaluation is not about assessment centers, paper-and-pencil tests, or 360-degree models; it is about caring and helping others become important links in a chain of success. Love is lost when personnel evaluation systems are designed to prove incompetence, rather than improve performance.

The Power of Love in Judging Others

Evaluating with love means that the evaluator does not unconditionally condone poor work performance; it means that the person is loved despite the unacceptable work habits. The quality of the product and quality of those producing it are the ingredients of evaluation systems. If "Quality Is Job One" for the Ford company, then a quality automobile is directly tied to a quality workforce composed of individual workers who feel valued and loved.

Remember the vision statement of the Hallmark company given in Chapter 2—"when you care enough to send the very best"? This caring is modeled by each artist, poet, market specialist, and manager every day. Hallmark employees view themselves as Hallmark Associates and evaluate each other's performance to help increase the joy they bring to customers who purchase and receive their products. This respect for individual contributions to the final product is reflected in Hallmark's leadership picture on the cover of the annual report. It is a picture of hundreds standing in a green field near corporate headquarters. Every person is an executive with Hallmark.

Management genius Max DePree (1989) of Herman Miller, Inc., created an exemplary performance evaluation system to help control the variance in job roles and to respect the people in them. Because no person in Herman Miller knows everything about the organization and each employee, DePree relied on love and trust. Depree explains his success this way: "We must trust one another to be accountable for our own assignments. When that kind of trust is present, it is a beautifully liberating thing" (p. 116). His evaluation philosophy was played out as he reviewed the performance of the senior management team. As part of the company "covenantal relationship," he asked that every member of the team review the performance of the people he or she leads.

DePree created a few questions that he asked his senior management team to consider:

- Would you be willing to share your philosophy of management with your work team?
- What are a few of the things that you expect most and need most from the CEO?
- Does Herman Miller need you?
- Do you need Herman Miller?
- What two things should we do to work toward being a great company?
- In the past year, what, from the perspective of integrity, most affected you personally, professionally, and organizationally? (pp. 117-120)

These questions were value added and modeled by DePree to guide each manager and line worker in the Herman Miller company. Great organizations such as Herman Miller have established a culture of trust, personal responsibility, and a way of treating all persons with respect for the job they do and the persons they are. This is the essence of the power of love in evaluating another person and oneself.

Quality and the *Love* Word

Quality has become the buzzword of the new century in organizations ranging from the IRS to the church house. "Continuous improvement" and "quality assurance" sound better than "TQM" because its checkered success in organizations failed to follow TQM principles. This explains why the movement has created suspicion among subordinates who believe that TQM is merely another management fad that will crumble under its own weight. TQM failures are usually caused by lack of leadership from the top and poor communication about its intent. W. Edwards Deming (1986) believed that continuous improvement and evaluation of products and personnel must be closely linked if benchmarks, visions, and missions are to be realized.

Jim "Mattress Mac" McIngvale used his persistence and the teachings of Deming to build Gallery Furniture Company in Houston, Texas, to annual sales of more than $180 million in 17 years. McIngvale moved to Houston in 1984 and, with only $5,000, started his furniture business. When the bottom fell out of the market in the early 1990s, Mac spent most his meager profits on television advertising that became well-known for his enthusiastic words, "Gallery Furniture really will save you money!" while waving dollar bills above his head. His risk taking and self-confidence paid off after he attended numerous seminars conducted by the late Edwards Deming. McIngvale applied the Deming principles of constancy of purpose, statistical quality control, and customer satisfaction to build the most successful furniture business in America. He models his words of customer service, continuous improvement, and thorough evaluation of every detail. An entrepreneur and a community leader, Mattress Mac is tireless in working with schools and other youth agencies to promote education, the work ethic, and healthy life styles.

As CEO of General Electric, Jack Welch initiated a combination of quality circles, TQM, site-based decision making, and transformational leadership to reform his company. The first day on the job, Welch began changing the old mind-set of corporate "priesthood" privileges to an egalitarian merit model based on measures of both quantity and quality. He believed the old adage that "every tub must sit on its own bottom" and challenged each of the 350,000 employees to meet the needs of customers every day and every minute. Employees were given the freedom to "think outside the box" to keep GE competitive and among the top *Fortune* 500 companies, but in the same vein, Welch informed them that all 350,000 employees were to be ranked each year on the basis of their performance records. Competition is part of Welch's evaluation formula to inspire high productivity in the company. Competition is the nature of Jack Welch.

In an interview on CBS's *60 Minutes,* a GE associate told about challenging Welch to a Ping-Pong game. In the heat of the contest, both Welch and his associate were diving into the hedges near the table to save errant shots and gain the upper hand. Thus, where does the love force come in with Welch and other highly competitive CEOs? Welch believes in annual evaluations of all GE employees on the basis of their performance and ranking them first to last. The bottom 10% are dismissed from the company.

How can GE or any organization rank personnel and provide incentive pay for some and fire the bottom 10%? According to Welch and other corporate leaders, by outplacing or firing the lowest performers, employers are doing them a favor. Welch believes that it is unloving to allow persons to flounder and fail each day and retain their jobs. It is management's duty to inform the employees to find jobs for which they are better suited and that would bring them more joy in their work and personal lives. Management authorities call Welch America's leading corporate executive. Executives throughout the world model his combination of hard-driving competition, personnel evaluation policies, and compassion for personnel.

The Baldrige Criteria
and Peak Performance

Love can easily fade, however, in highly competitive organizations in which profit is the *raison d'être* at the expense of employees and customers. When profit drives everything else, no management system will work. Continuous improvement or TQM, properly implemented, can propel organizations to peak performance when management takes the long view, rather than the quick fix, toward organizational change. It is unrealistic to believe that TQM can work magic in a few weeks or months or to believe that all organizations have made TQM work.

Developed to provide guidance to high performance, the Baldrige criteria for continuous improvement are based on research and best practice in private and public organizations. In industry, Dow Chemical, Motorola, and Ford and in education, the Brazosport Independent School District (Texas) are examples of the power of the Baldrige criteria in guiding organizational choices toward excellence. These organizations used the Malcolm Baldrige Award guidelines as a model. The seven key requirements are as follows:

1. The introduction of quality products and services, emphasizing how processes are designed to meet or exceed customer requirements
2. Process and quality controls that assume that the products and systems meet design specifications
3. Continuous improvement techniques (controlled experiments, evaluation of new technology, and benchmarking) and methods of integrating them
4. Quality assessments of process, products, services, and practices
5. Documentation

6. Quality assurance, quality assessment, and quality improvement of support services and business processes (accounting, sales, purchasing, personnel, etc.)
7. Quality assurance, quality assessment, and quality improvement of suppliers (audits, inspections, certifications, testing, partnerships, training, incentives, and recognition)

According to Hubbard (1996), "Once a company is satisfied that an effective quality system has been established, it might be desirable to examine the Baldrige Award criteria on subsequent years to see if the goals of business excellence and quality achievement are likely met" (p. 25). The emphasis on improving the system, rather than blaming the employee, not only is the key to high performance but also sends a positive signal about the worth and dignity of individuals. This is love in action.

Love Takes Time to Work in Food Safety

Mohammed, a food safety supervisor employed by the U.S. Department of Agriculture (USDA), was a recent student of mine in a graduate seminar on coaching and mentoring at Texas A&M University. The course is part of the new Supervisor Education Program (SEP) for food safety specialists in red meat and poultry processing plants. Course content is designed to advance the knowledge and skill levels of the supervisors to meet the new Hazard Analysis and Critical Control Point system (HACCP) to reduce *E. coli, Salmonella,* and other pathogens in food products. The training consists of lectures and lab work in the natural and social sciences directly related to the supervisors' job responsibilities.

During a lecture on the merits of quality coaching, mentoring, and team leadership, Mohammed raised his hand and said, "But professor, you don't understand. This is really good material, but you are preaching to the choir. Our hands are tied in using these mentoring and coaching skills in our plants." I asked why. Mohammed replied,

In my chicken processing plant, we are told by the USDA that food inspection accountability has been delegated to each plant to better meet HACCP guidelines. I find that the union protects the production line workers, and management ignores me because they must respond to pressures from the plant owners and stockholders to increase profits. When I try to coach the line worker, the union representative tells me to back off; when I say something to an inspector, a company employee, he or she resents suggestions from me; and the most troubling is when I suspect a pathogen problem and attempt to slow down production, then management tells me to "stop whining and push more birds to market."

Mohammed agrees that he knows what his job is and has the necessary resources to do his job, but he rarely gets any praise for his work and doesn't get the respect he should have as a doctor of veterinary medicine. He told the class and me that the greatest problem is that

> this course material needs to be taught to top-level USDA bureaucrats, plant managers, and owners. If supervisors are the conscience of the plant to ensure HACCP compliance, then we need more authority and respect to evaluate the quality of employees handing the food and judging the quality of stock coming into the slaughter plants, and greater authority over the quality of each package of chicken shipped from the plant.

This outburst of frustration by Mohammed was supported by nods of agreement by others in the class. My response to them was about how change is usually a painful experience, especially when the rules of accountability are changed. Because the USDA was striving to implement the new guidelines and reduce foodborne pathogens, they have attempted to decentralize both the responsibility and the authority over red meat and poultry production.

They were following sound recommendations by Rosabeth Kanter and other management gurus who recommend that the best management is less management from the top because those closest to the production of red meat and chicken should be empowered with the authority, the resources, and the rewards for better, safer products. With time, patience, leadership in the USDA, and the commitment of stockholders and owners to safer products, the decentralized model will succeed. The process of changing to transformational leadership is slow, however, and may take a generation of new "out of the box" managers to change to a workplace in which love drives respect and quality.

I tell the students that regardless of the obstacles they encounter, they are the heart and soul of each plant in guiding others to pathogen-free products. They are the guardians of the quality of each chicken or hamburger patty that winds up on our plates each day. They are the scientists with the training who must become better communicators, team builders, coaches, critical thinkers, and moral leaders who allow love to rule over the chaotic and uncaring world that other employees see in the processing plants.

High-Stakes Tests and Love for Students

High-stakes tests have become embedded in our education systems. The SAT, ACT, and other exams have ruled university admissions for 25 years. High test scores are the key to admission and scholarships to elite institutions, and lower scores are used to either bar students from higher education or force them to apply to less prestigious schools. The argument to eliminate the SAT, ACT, and other entrance exams is growing. The exams are viewed as antiquated instruments that fail to measure the intellectual capacities of many students, especially those of color and low-economic status. Others argue that the "best and brightest" are students with top test scores who are ready for the rigors of university study, whereas those with lower scores are doomed to failure. Universities that have eliminated the use of the SAT or ACT have turned to measures relevant to actual course work and job expectations. Research findings about the SAT and ACT indicate that students from affluent backgrounds score higher than do those from middle- and lower-income homes.

It is obvious to me that admission to higher education has been ruled by high-stakes tests too long and that other measures, for example, high school success on college preparatory courses, class rankings, desire, creativity, leadership, and integrity, are superior predictors of success in the university and in life. Entrance exams make student selection much easier for university officials; if higher education is to serve all America's youth, however, then admission procedures must be guided by love to ensure diversity and equal opportunity.

High-stakes tests for high school graduation are the law in 18 states, and other states will soon join the national trend ("Seeking Stability," 2001). The use of statewide high-stakes tests evoke either high praise or condemnation from legislators, teachers, principals, scholars, parents, and students. Accountability for performance has proved to be both a blessing and a curse, depending on how well students perform on state-mandated tests in math, science, language arts, reading, and writing. Testing authority Scott Thompson (2001) calls the high-stakes test the "evil twin" of authentic, student-centered school reform.

School administrators and teachers know the value of a caring and loving school climate but live under a blanket of fear caused by school rankings based on students' performance on state-mandated examinations. Students in 18 states cannot graduate from high school if they fail to pass the exam in the 11th or 12th grade. The good news is that these high-stakes tests have been a major factor in school reform efforts in several states, with Texas and North Carolina leading the way. Minority and lower-income children have made noticeable improvements as a result of aligning and teaching the curriculum directed toward test items. A worst-case scenario on the evils of high-stakes test competition happened in a high-wealth school district in the Houston, Texas, area. A second-grade teacher gave the following account:

> One afternoon at 2:30 p.m., the faculty at Meadow Grove Elementary School received an e-mail message from the superintendent of schools. They were told to be on time in the auditorium at 3:30 p.m. for a meeting with him and his central office staff. In his words, "Something terrible has happened, and we need to do something about it." The second-grade teacher and her colleagues thought that there must have been a shooting or at least a gun found in the school, or someone had stolen money from the school activity fund. At 3:30, the faculty and office staff gathered in the school auditorium to face a grim superintendent. He began, "I have just received word today that this school has embarrassed the school board and the district. You have let us down by falling from the 'exemplary' to the 'recognized' category. This is the first time a school under my watch has dropped from the state's highest ranking. What are we going to tell our community about your failure?"

The second-grade teacher telling the story said she could not believe what was occurring and wanted to laugh but realized the serious tone of the meeting. She knew that only five third-grade students had failed to master the math portion of the Texas Assessment of Academic Skills (TAAS) test. This small number caused the school to drop to "recognized" status. Some of the teachers began crying and hugging each other to deal with the situation, and others were stunned by event.

Where is love in this school? The pressure placed on the superintendent and handed down to each campus, rather than teaching and caring for each child and each other, had become the driving force. Evaluation without considering the values of people who compose the system becomes a weapon to hold people hostage, rather than a guide to help them sustain a constancy of purpose and self-esteem.

Because more states are requiring students to pass the high-stakes test to graduate from high school, questions are growing about the impact of a single test on the future lives of these students. The tests are becoming more difficult because they are based on rigorous university preparation curricula. In time, these higher standards could prove successful in preparing more students for higher education, but current students caught in the curriculum-test gap in large urban school districts are sensing futility in passing the new exams and are dropping out at a rate of 30% to 50%.

Where is the love in this system? Reformers respond with a tough-love answer—"Love without rigor and high standards is not acceptable. Students will respond to the demands we place on them." For some reason, this popular answer rings hollow for many children and youth caught in circumstances beyond their control. Studies by Skrla and Scheurich (2001), however, find convincing evidence that the Texas school accountability movement driven by the TAAS has increased the achievement of children of color and those from lower-income homes. They challenge the position of Rice University researcher Linda McNeil (2000), who provides a convincing argument that overemphasis on the TAAS forces schools to narrow the curriculum and restrict the overall learning of children from lower-income families. One of America's leading scholars on school improvement, Tom Sergiovanni (2000), puts high-stakes testing in the proper perspective:

> When state-mandated standards and high-stakes tests are part of a larger system of accountability that includes local standards and local assessment, they are more likely to be helpful in holding schools accountable and in helping schools get better than is now the case. Used alone, I fear, mandated standards and tests provide a dangerously narrow approach to accountability. (p. 6)

Sonny Donaldson is a recently retired superintendent of Aldine, a large urban Texas school district with 82% minority enrollment and more than 70% of those qualifying for free or reduced lunches. Donaldson used the TAAS and his love for students to lead the district to high student performance and self-esteem. He told the community, school board, and teachers that there are "no excuses" for children of color or from poverty to fail in the Aldine schools. He stressed that what gets measured gets taught and that high-stakes test scores are critical to the student and district success.

His love for each student was the benchmark to lead the Aldine district to success and brought hope to the lives of thousands of children and youth. Thus, tests have their place in evaluating the performance of individuals but only if other measures are included to help ensure equitable opportunities for everyone.

Profit Over Patients

Management told a hospital administrator that she must shorten the stay of patients in the hospital as a cost-saving measure. She was told,

"Outpatients need only one day's stay unless they are in ICU or other intensive care units." Data-driven management knew that increased numbers of patients undergoing surgery meant more profit to the bottom line. Doctors, nurses, and other medical team members were outraged by the reduced stay policy for patients but felt powerless because management controlled their salaries and benefits.

Two patients who underwent gallstone "day surgery" and became ill at home after a one-day hospital stay sought legal advice but found that they had no case because the policy was in place before they had surgery. Several young mothers pushed from the hospital after two days were unable to find adequate health care at home and found no one who would take their complaints to the hospital administrator. When a husband of one of the young mothers confronted the administrator, she said,

> I only do what management tells me to do. This hospital must make a profit to survive, and it is the only hospital within 70 miles of here. We reduce hospital stay for what we believe is sound policy and in the best interest of patients.

Where is the love in this hospital? The vision statement for the hospital reads, "Watson Medical Center Hospital is patient-centered and dedicated to providing quality medical care for all patients." Is something wrong here? Is the profit more important than providing each patient with the best health care?

Love in the Air

The airline industry has responded to federal regulations and intense competition by increasing the number of flights; adding seats but little luggage space to accommodate more passengers; reducing the quality and frequency of meals; and overbooking, canceling, and delaying flights. As a result, air rage among passengers has become more frequent. Business travelers constantly complain that air travel becomes a greater hassle each year. Efforts are under way by American, Delta, Continental, and other major carriers to add more legroom, reduce the number of delays, respond more quickly to ticket problems, and improve communication with customers.

Jan, a Continental flight attendant, should be consulted by management about servant leadership. Jan modeled her servant leadership on a full flight from Baltimore to Houston when she discovered that a mother and her daughter with physical disabilities were separated by two rows.

Before departure, Jan told the mother that she would try to get them seated together because the daughter had special needs.

In a loud but pleasing voice, Jan asked if anyone would be so kind as to change seats to unite mother and daughter. No one moved or appeared to hear her plea. Undaunted, Jan turned to a tired gentleman sitting in an aisle seat and asked if he would agree to change seats because the center seat next to him was vacant. Jan's beautiful, authentic smile touched a kind spot in the man's heart. He immediately stood up, walked up two rows, and invited and assisted the young girl to his former seat. He told the mother that "thanks to Jan, you can now sit together."

Love won once again, in a crowded, uncomfortably warm plane waiting for takeoff in Baltimore. I wonder if anyone reported Jan's act of kindness and included it in her annual performance evaluation? Evaluation of the bottom line is important to guide schools to high performance, help hospitals heal people, and keep airlines flying, but evaluation without love leads to measurement without meaning. A vision for evaluation based on customer satisfaction has often been blinded by the bright lights of peak performance and profit.

Leading With Love While Evaluating

Leading with love while evaluating performance means far more than applying the tools of evaluation. The force of love works if the evaluation tools are used to help the organization and each individual improve his or her job performance. The value-added action by top management to evaluate and improve the system, rather than punish the employee or the client, is the focus of continuous improvement. It is folly to install a personnel evaluation process in isolation of the system. The system must be transformed to be employee and customer focused.

To blame employees for the failures in the organization is tantamount to blaming the defensive unit of a football team for the inept performance of the offense. War hero General George Patton understood how the system restricts individual initiative and performance. During the battle for the Rhine River in the winter of 1945, Patton wrote a letter to his superior, General Omar Bradley, saying, "All the U.S. troops except the Third Army were doing nothing at all, and that while I was attacking, I could do better with more divisions . . ." (Ambrose, 1997, p. 412). Philosopher Kahlil Gibran (1964) knew the values of work and self-evaluation. He wrote, "Work is love made visible. And if you cannot work with love but only with distaste, it is better that you should sit at the gate of the temple and take alms of those who work with joy" (p. 28).

When the system fails the workers, the workers fail the system and find no joy or love in their endeavors. The landmark work of Frederick Herzberg (1968), Victor Vroom (1964), and others built the theoretical foundation of motivation for Edwards Deming (1986) and his many disciples. Herzberg found that the motivators included trust, personal achievement, the work itself, and recognition. If the system stifles individual initiative with poor working conditions, weak leadership by management, and unrealistic rules and policies, however, no personnel evaluation system will be accurate to judge individual performance. Vroom found that if the organization sends negative signals with inadequate performance assessments and if the workers see no incentive for working hard and learning skills to become better performers, they will either leave or merely get by to earn a paycheck.

Paul Hersey and Ken Blanchard (1988) made significant contributions to improving worker performance by using situational leadership. They combined motivational research with systemic change to produce a model to guide the actions of organizational leaders. If personnel are producing at higher levels, the system is working to satisfy employees. Hersey and Blanchard reasoned that employees perform below par for three basic reasons: one, they are not committed to the job itself; two, they lack the job skills; and three, management has not inspired and coached them to become part of the organizational culture.

If the employees lack the skills, management must assess the skill levels and provide training. Unskilled and nonmotivated employees are immature workers and therefore must be taught the skills necessary to become successful. When the training manifests itself in higher performance, management pushes harder on the vision and purpose of the organization and its products. Then managers use their skills of persuasion to sell the employees on the importance of their tasks to the overall success of the organization and for themselves. The art of evaluating with love must be a delicate balance of love for others and the pursuit of the highest quality for every product every day.

Models for Evaluating Organizations and the People in Them

As discussed above, companies, schools, universities, and other organizations are involved in total quality and continuous improvement. Corporate executives, school superintendents, and military commanders are encouraging their charges to use affinity diagrams, fishbone diagrams, flowcharting, histograms, run charts, control charts, lotus diagrams, relations diagrams, praeto diagrams, plus/delta charts, the PDSA (plan, do, study, act) cycle, and force field analysis. CEOs who catch the quality fever try to infect employees in hopes of improving all aspects of the production process.

John Conyers (2000), superintendent of the Community Consolidated School District in Palatine, Illinois, was introduced to the total quality concept by Motorola's chief executive officer, who credited total quality as "the single most important measure of the company's success and related how Motorola developed its Six Sigma criteria as a structure for achieving the highest possible level of quality across the entire organization" (p. 22). Conyers took this message and applied total quality to his school district. In a short time, he found decreases in student misbehavior incidents, reductions in errors in student work, and increases in the completion and quality of homework. Other school districts take the same steps and reap few successes. Why do continuous improvement models work in some organizations and fail in others? It is love and belief in people that make the system work.

All organizations need to establish quality measures that go beyond end-of-year profit margins. Organizations, whether for-profit or nonprofit, are made up of individuals. Profit organizations, such as GE, Texaco, Wal-Mart, and Joe's hot dog stand, survive through satisfied customer sales and the buying habits of the public. Nonprofit organizations, such as schools, universities, fraternities, the Red Cross, and churches, must rely on public funding, private support, and memberships. To succeed in either category, they must be customer or client centered.

Corporations that make the *Fortune* 500 Top 20 sometimes forget that their buying customers and employees pushed them to the top. Once management forgets customer satisfaction and employee empowerment, the fall from the heights is certain. This explains why more than 40% of the top 100 *Fortune* 500 companies change every five years.

Major corporations such as General Motors, Ford Motor Company, Microsoft, McDonald's, Wal-Mart Stores, and AOL Time Warner are vast enterprises with layers of personnel, franchises, and products that make organizational assessment complex. Large state universities, urban school districts, the United Way, the Salvation Army, and the Internal Revenue Service are no less difficult to evaluate. But quality assessment systems must be in place to respond quickly to customer habits and behaviors and to market trends. The system, however, is only as good as those making judgments about the data. Customer-sensitive, site-based organizations can respond to change more rapidly than top-down, CEO-based entities. Automobile sales rest on the ability of top management to analyze consumer likes and dislikes, make quick decisions, and rely on the creativity of designers to meet those demands. The quality of school systems is based on the ability of superintendents, central office officials, and building principals to analyze student test scores, disaggregate and make the test data available to teachers, and rely on their creativity to analyze the test data and make needed adjustments to instructional strategies.

How to Evaluate With Love

Almost all employees want to do a good job. A performance evaluation system that is responsive to their needs will inspire them and provide professional development to help them improve each year. Caring managers and administrators must always be aware that performance appraisals are stressful under the best conditions and that under the worst conditions, they will destroy morale. Employees want to know how they are doing in the eyes of their bosses and seek ways to improve their skills and performance. If employees are the top priority, then the system in which they work needs continuous evaluation to ensure the best working conditions possible.

Expectations of peak performance and high standards are morale boosters when people know how to do the job and are given encouragement by every person in the organization. The groundbreaking work of Buckingham and Coffman (1999) leads to powerful questions about employee needs. Their work drew on 25 years of research conducted by the Gallup Organization that asked more than a million employees, "What do the most talented employees need from their workplace?" From these data, Buckingham and Coffman found this:

> Talented employees need great managers. The talented employee may join a company because of its charismatic leaders, its generous benefits, and its world-class training programs, but how long that employee stays and how productive he is there is determined by his relationship with his immediate supervisor. (pp. 11-12)

Buckingham and Coffman (1999) found that the following six questions revealed the most important information from employees in all types of organizations:

1. Do I know what is expected of me at work?
2. Do I have the materials and equipment I need to do my best work right?

3. At work, do I have the opportunity to do what I do best every day?
4. In the last seven days, have I received recognition and praise for doing good work?
5. Does my supervisor, or someone at work, seem to care about me as a person?
6. Is there someone at work who encourages my work? (p. 34)

How, then, can you as leader-manager use the ideas in these six questions to make personnel evaluation a path to growth and job satisfaction that ensures that love will lead all employees to be better than they think they can be? The following suggestions for successful personnel evaluations are drawn from recent research and best practice in all types of organizations. Compare these suggestions with your current practices of personnel evaluation and see if an idea or two emerges.

1. Does the organizational vision statement inspire cooperation and excellence? Does the statement energize others to perform at higher levels of success and hope for the future? Does the vision statement inspire a belief that employees know what to do, know how to do it, want to do it, and receive praise and recognition from their supervisor for doing it? If the vision statement is unclear or lacks inspiration, rework the words until the statement is clear, compelling, and owned by everyone.

2. Ask each employee to write six or seven specific goals directly related to the vision statement with job skills and processes that he or she will use to facilitate and complete the tasks.

3. Schedule a 30-minute meeting with each employee and his or her immediate supervisor to share the goals, job skills, and processes that the employee needs to successfully meet each goal. During the meeting, give positive recognition, praise the abilities of each person, and say that you will do your best to provide the materials, assistance, and training to ensure each person's success in accomplishing each goal. Express to them that the vision of the organization seeks excellence in the product being produced, the student being taught, or the patient being treated. This excellence guides the "cause greater than ourselves," and the final evaluation of the product is its value to the customer.

4. Become visible at workstations, and spend time observing and commenting on the positive work going on. After a few visits, the fear of being viewed as the enemy or "snoopervisor" will disappear. The number of times is not as important as the types of questions you ask related to the six questions listed above. Open communication and trust are the cor-

nerstones of solid staff evaluation. The love factor is the cement that holds the cornerstones in place.

5. Schedule a 30-minute session with each employee at least four times a year. Ask employees if they are clear in their understanding about knowing what to do, if they have the necessary material and training to do it, and what the immediate supervisor could do to make the job more appealing and challenging. Tell the employees to keep the vision for the best possible product and to ask for help, offer praise for their accomplishments, and tell them that they are winning team members. Evaluation and clear benchmarks are keys to high-flying organizations, but without love, the flight will be short-lived.

I'll close this chapter with the powerful words of Mother Teresa (1995) about the power of love in inspiring others to greater accomplishments.

What we need is love without getting tired. How does a lamp burn? Through the continuous input of small drops of oil. What are these drops of oil in our lamps? They are the small things of daily life: faithfulness, small words of kindness, a thought for others, our way of being silent, of looking, of speaking, and of acting. (p. 22)

References

Albom, M. (1997). *Tuesdays with Morrie.* New York: Doubleday.

Aldrich, M. (2000, August 2). Daring to care. *Bryan-College Station Eagle,* pp. D1-D2.

Ambrose, S. (1997). *Citizen soldiers.* New York: Touchstone.

Arrien, A. (1998). Introduction. In A. Arrien (Ed.), *Working together: Producing synergy by honoring diversity* (pp. 1-11). Pleasanton, CA: New Leaders Press.

Autry, H. (1992). *Love and profit: The art of caring leadership.* New York: Avon.

Barker, J. (1992). *Paradigms: The business of discovering the future.* New York: HarperBusiness.

Barnard, C. I. (1968). *Functions of the executive* (30th ann. ed.). Cambridge, MA: Harvard University Press. (Original work published 1938)

Berry, L. (1995). *On great service: A framework for action.* New York: Free Press.

Block, P. (1993). *Stewardship: Choosing service over self-interest.* San Francisco: Berrett-Koehler.

Bolman, L., & Deal, T. (1993). *Leading with soul: An uncommon journey of spirit.* San Francisco: Jossey-Bass.

Booher, D. (2000). *Communication with confidence.* New York: McGraw-Hill.

Brown, H., & Spizman, R. (1996). *A hero in every heart.* Nashville, TN: Thomas Nelson.

Brownlow, L. (1972). *Today is mine.* Fort Worth, TX: Brownlow.

Buckingham, M., & Clifton, D. (2001). *Now, discover your strengths.* New York: Free Press.

Buckingham, M., & Coffman, C. (1999). *First, break all the rules.* New York: Simon & Schuster.

Canada, B. (2000). What kind of leader are you? *School Administrator, 57*(8), 56.

Carlson, R. (1998). *Don't sweat the small stuff at work.* New York: Hyperion.

Caudron, S. (2000). Building better bosses. *Workforce, 79*(5), 33-39.

Cessna, R. (2000, Sept. 29). Coach left good sons, memories. *Bryan-College Station Eagle,* p. I5.

Clancy, H. (2001, March 25). Teachers' legacy seen in students. *Bryan-College Station Eagle,* p. D1.

Clifton, D., & Nelson, P. (1992). *Soar with your strengths.* New York: Dell.

Collie, A. (2000, December 2). Riley takes the heat. *American Way,* pp. 110-111.

Conyers, J. (2000). When status quo won't do. *School Administrator, 57*(6), 22-27.

Covey, S. (1990). *Principle-centered leadership.* New York: Simon & Schuster.

Cunningham, W. (1991). *Empowerment: Vitalizing personal energy.* Atlanta, GA: Humantics New Age.

Cutlip, S., Center, A., & Broom, G. (1985). *Effective public relations.* Englewood Cliffs, NJ: Prentice Hall.

Daft, R. (1983). *Organizational theory and design.* St. Paul, MN: West.

Davis, K. (1978). Overlord: The Allies triumph in Normandy. In *Reader's Digest illustrated history of World War II* (pp. 346-357). New York: Reader's Digest Association.

Decker, B. (1992). *You've got to be believed to be heard.* New York: St. Martin's.

Deming, W. E. (1986). *Out of the crisis.* Cambridge: MIT, Center for Advanced Engineering Study.

DePree, M. (1989). *Leadership is an art.* Des Plaines, IL: Dell.

Dreher, G., & Ash, R. (1990). A comparative study of mentoring among men and women in managerial, professional, and technical positions. *Journal of Applied Psychology, 75*(5), 539-546.

Drucker, P. (1985). *The effective manager.* New York: HarperBusiness.

Drucker, P. (1994). *Post-capitalist society.* New York: HarperBusiness.

Dyer, W. (1998). *Wisdom of the ages.* New York: HarperCollins.

Edelman, M. (1992). *The measure of our success.* Boston: Beacon.

Feinstein, J. (1996). *Civil war: Army vs. Navy.* Boston: Little, Brown.

Follett, M. P. (1930). *Creative experience.* London: Longmans, Green.

Frankl, V. (1984). *Man's search for meaning.* New York: Washington Square.

Fulghum, R. (1989). *All I really need to know I learned in kindergarten.* New York: Villard.

Gibran, K. (1964). *The prophet.* New York: Knopf.

Gilbert, L., & Rossman, K. (1992). Gender and the mentoring process for women: Implications for professional development. *Professional Psychology: Research and Practice, 23*(3), 233-238.

Goldfarb, J. (1991). *The cynical society.* Chicago: University of Chicago Press.

Goldhaber, G. (1974). *Organizational communication.* Dubuque, IA: William C. Brown.

Goleman, D. (1997). *Emotional intelligence: Why it can matter more than IQ.* New York: Bantam.

Greenleaf, R. (1991). *Servant leadership: A journey into the nature of legitimate power and greatness.* Mahwah, NJ: Paulist.

Guion, R. (1998). *Assessment, measurement, and production of personnel decisions.* Mahwah, NJ: Lawrence Erlbaum.

Haddock, B. (1998). Flowering of the narcissus. *Haddock Letter, 8*(2), 5.

Henricks, M. (2001, February 15). Positions of strengths. *American Way,* pp. 105-109.

Hersey, P., & Blanchard, K. (1988). *Management of organizational behavior: Utilizing human resources* (5th ed.). Englewood Cliffs, NJ: Prentice Hall.

Herzberg, F. (1968, January-February). One more time: How do you motivate employees? *Harvard Business Review, 46*(1), 53-62.

Hogan, K. (2000). *Talk your way to the top.* Gretna, LA: Pelican.

Hoyle, J. (1995). *Leadership and futuring: Making visions happen.* Thousand Oaks, CA: Corwin.

Hoyle, J., English, F., & Steffy, B. (1998). *Skills for successful 21st century school leaders: Standards for peak performers.* Arlington, VA: American Association of School Administrators.

Hoyle, J., & Oates, A. (1998). Principals' interpersonal sensitivity toward teachers, central office personnel, parents, business leaders, and community members. In R. Muth & M. Martin (Eds.), *Toward the year 2000: Leadership by quality schools* (6th yearbook of the National Council of Professors of Educational Administration, pp. 148-157). Lancaster, PA: Technomic.

Hoyle, J., & Skrla, L. (1999). The politics of superintendent evaluation. *Journal of Educational Personnel Evaluation, 13*(4), 405-419.

Hoyle, J., & Slater, R. (2001, June). Love, happiness, and America's schools: The role of educational leadership in the 21st century. *Phi Delta Kappan, 82*(10), 790-794.

Hubbard, M. (1996). *Statistical quality control for the food industry.* New York: Chapman & Hall.

Janka, G. (1998). Getting to know you. In A. Arrien (Ed.), *Working together: Producing synergy by honoring diversity* (pp. 41-59). Pleasanton, CA: New Leaders Press.

Jowett, B. (1871). *The dialogues of Plato.* Boston: Jefferson Press.

Kanter, R. (1979, July-August). Power failure in management circuits. *Harvard Business Review, 57*(4), 65-75.

Kikoski, J., & Kikoski, C. (1996). *Reflexive communication in the culturally diverse workplace.* Westport, CT: Quorum.

Kouzes, J., & Posner, B. (1993). *Credibility.* San Francisco: Jossey-Bass.

Kouzes, J., & Posner, B. (1995). *The leadership challenge.* San Francisco: Jossey-Bass.

Kouzes, J., & Posner, B. (1996). Envisioning our future: Imagining ideal scenarios. *Futurist, 30*(3), 14-19.

Krohn, P. (1999). *The Maggid speaks: Favorite stories and parables of Rabbi Sholom Schwadron.* Brooklyn, NY: Mesorah.

Lewis, L. (2001). *The effect of gender on an induction year mentoring program for principals as perceived by selected female principals and their mentors in Austin, Texas.* Unpublished dissertation, Texas A&M University, College Station.

Luhabe, W. N. (1998). Bridging the gap. In A. Arrien (Ed.), *Working together: Producing synergy by honoring diversity* (pp. 73-83). Pleasanton, CA: New Leaders Press.

Machiavelli, N. (1984). *The prince.* Harmondsworth, UK: Penguin.

Maddux, R. (2000). *Effective performance appraisal* (4th ed.). Menlo Park, CA: Crisp.

Malone, P. (1986). *Love 'em and lead 'em.* Annandale, VA: Synergy Press.

Manners, G., & Steger, J. (1979). The implications of research on the R&D manager's role to the selection and training of scientists and engineers for management. *R&D Management, 9,* 85-92.

Marcic, D. (1997). *Managing with the wisdom of love: Uncovering virtue in people and organizations.* San Francisco: Jossey-Bass.

Marshall, C., Patterson, J., Rogers, D., & Steele, J. (1996). Caring as career: An alternative perspective for educational administration. *Educational Administration Quarterly, 32*(2), 271-294.

Martin, D. (1994). *TeamThink: Using the sports connection to develop, motivate, and manage a winning business team.* New York: Dutton/Plume.

McCann, J., & Kaminsky, P. (1998). *Stop and sell the roses.* New York: Ballantine.

McClelland, D. (1978). The two faces of power. In D. Hampton, C. Summer, & R. Webber (Eds.), *Organizational behavior and the practice of management.* Glenview, IL: Scott, Foresman.

McGregor, D. (1964). *The human side of enterprise.* New York: McGraw-Hill.

McNeil, L. (2000). Creating new inequalities. *Phi Delta Kappan, 81*(10), 729-734.

Meharbian, A. (1971). *Silent message.* Belmont, CA: Wadsworth.

Merriam-Webster's collegiate dictionary (10th ed.) (1993). Springfield, MA: Merriam-Webster.

Mertz, N., Welch, D., & Henderson, J. (1990). *Executive mentoring.* Newton, MA: WEEB.

Moore, T. (1992). *Care of the soul.* New York: HarperCollins.

Mother Teresa. (1995). *No greater love.* Novato, CA: New World Library.

Nichols, W. (1962). *Words to live by.* New York: Simon & Schuster.

Olofson, C. (2001, February 1). Just the meaningful facts. *American Way,* p. 64.

Osborne, D., & Gaebler, T. (1992). *Reinventing government: How the entrepreneurial spirit is transforming the public sector.* Reading, MA: Addison-Wesley.

Pinchot, G., III. (1985). *Intrapreneuring.* New York: Harper & Row.

Public Gas Association. (2001). *Public Gas News, 20*(2), 2.

Ragins, R., & Sundstrom, E. (1989). Gender and power in organizations: A longitudinal perspective. *Psychological Bulletin, 105*(1), 51-88.

Robbins, H., & Finley, M. (1998). *Transcompetition: Moving beyond competition and collaboration.* New York: McGraw-Hill.

Rogers, J. (1986). *Winston Churchill.* New York: Chelsea House.

Roget's international thesaurus (New ed., 21st printing). (1961). New York: Crowell.

Ryan, M. (2000, October 29). This is medicine the way it should be. *Parade Magazine,* pp. 18-19.

Sanford, K. (1998). *Leading with love: How women and men can transform their organizations through maternalistic management.* Olalla, WA: Vashon.

Schleier, C. (2000). An unforgettable fire. *TCU Magazine, 44*(3), 16-23.

Schmitt, N., & Cohen, S. (1990). *Criterion-related and content validity of the NASSP Assessment Center.* Reston, VA: National Association of Secondary School Principals.

Seeking stability for standards-based education: Executive summary. (2001). *Education Week, 20*(17), 8-9.

Sergiovanni, T. (1992). *Moral leadership: Getting to the heart of school improvement.* San Francisco: Jossey-Bass.

Sergiovanni, T. (2000). Standards and the lifeworld of leadership. *School Administrator, 57*(8), 6-12.

Seymour, P. (1979). *Moments bright and shining.* Norwalk, CT: C. R. Gibson.

Singh, R. (1998). *The path to tranquility.* New York: Viking Arkana.

Skrla, L., & Scheurich, J. (2001). Displacing deficit thinking in school district leadership. *Education and Urban Society, 33*(3), 235-259.

Spruell, G. (1985). Making it big time: Is it really tougher for women? *Training and Development Journal, 7,* 30-33.

Stallings, G., & Cook, S. (1997). *Another season.* Boston: Little, Brown.

Swindoll, C. (1991). *The inspirational writings of Charles Swindoll: Improving your serve.* New York: Inspirational Press.

Thompson, S. (2001). The authentic standards movement and its evil twin. *Phi Delta Kappan, 82*(5), 358-362.

Thornton, G., & Byham, W. (1983). *Assessment centers and managerial performance.* Orlando, FL: Academic Press.

Tichy, N., & Devanna, M. (1990). *The transformational leader.* New York: John Wiley.

Tichy, N., & Sherman, S. (1993). *Control your destiny or someone else will.* New York: Doubleday.

Tulgan, B. (2000). *Managing generation X.* New York: Norton.

Vroom, V. (1964). *Work and motivation.* New York: John Wiley.

Wasden, F. D. (1988). *The mentoring handbook.* Provo, UT: Brigham Young University, College of Education.

Index

The Corwin Press logo—a raven striding across an open book—represents the happy union of courage and learning. We are a professional-level publisher of books and journals for K-12 educators, and we are committed to creating and providing resources that embody these qualities. Corwin's motto is "Success for All Learners."